THE LIFE

ISSUES AS THEY PERTAIN TO THE SOUL

HENRY WILLIAMS JR.

ACW Press
Phoenix, Arizona 85013

The Essence of Life: Issues As They Pertain to the Soul
Copyright ©2001 Henry Williams, Jr.
All rights reserved

Cover design by Eric Walljasper
Interior design by Pine Hill Graphics

Packaged by ACW Press
5501 N. 7th Ave., #502
Phoenix, Arizona 85013
www.acwpress.com
The views expressed or implied in this work do not necessarily reflect those of ACW Press. Ultimate design, content, and editorial accuracy of this work is the responsibility of the author(s).

Publisher's Cataloging-in-Publication
(Provided by Quality Books, Inc.)

Williams, Henry, 1970-
    The essence of life : issues as they pertain to the
  soul / Henry Williams, Jr. -- 1st ed.
    p. cm.
    ISBN: 1-892525-52-6

    1. Spiritual life. 2. God--Knowableness. 3. God--Attributes. 4. Experience (Religion) I. Title.

BL53.W55 2001   291.4'4
                            QBI01-200418

All rights reserved. No part of this book may be reproduced, stored in a retrieval system, or transmitted in any form or by any means–electronic, mechanical, photocopying, recording, or otherwise–without prior permission in writing from the copyright holder except as provided by USA copyright law.

Printed in the United States of America by Bethany Press International, Bloomington, Minnesota 55438.

Dedication

I would like to dedicate this first of many books to come to my beloved God above who inspired every word of this influential writing. I then would like to give special attention to my lovely wife, Katrina, and our two beautiful daughters, Kristen and Lauren, and our new addition expected soon. They allowed me the time to hear the words of our creator and the support to launch out into unfamiliar territory. May the peace of God continue to abide over each of their lives and guide their every thought.

Table of Contents

Foreword 7
1. *The Beginning* 9
2. *Deception* 29
3. *Reality* 43
4. *God and Democracy* 49
5. *Fear, Doubt, and Unbelief* 59
6. *Idolatry* 69
7. *Love vs. Hate* 79
8. *The Past vs. the Present* 87
9. *The Heart: Mankind's Foundation of All Truths* 95
10. *The Bible* 109
11. *Prosperity: The Right to Succeed* 117
12. *The Mind: The Acknowledgment of Good and Evil* 127

Foreword

*I*t is very interesting that this book decribes a fight within each of us and our daily struggles to overcome obstacles that seem to influence our decisions and cloud our views. From the beginning, the author challenges our foundation of truths by insisting that we all have a common beginning that can only be found by our individual search for the beginning source of life. He maneuvers in such a way as if he is led by a force pulling him into every point that is revealed. Henry Williams is a talented orator which easily puts to paper what comes to mind. From chapter to chapter we see the personal challenges and the compromised truths that allow us to derive our own meaning of the truth and what it entails. This book is necessary for the world to read because it provides insights and revelations to common concerns. It doesn't attempt to answer every question for us, however, its intended purpose is to help us find the strength to answer our own questions for ourselves.

To know him is to not be surprised that such fluent words seep out of his heart and cause those close to him to embrace the truth. Although he is not as philosophical as this revelation presumes, the carefully chosen words do indeed articulate his character. In fact, you could say that *The Essence of Life* is a plotted course of his personal encounters, spiritually and humanly. The insight of this masterpiece is one that reaches out to all nationalities and races and cultures all across the world, not seeking to unite because of common struggles but connecting with each other through one source.

It is intriguing to get consumed by the sometimes philosophical views of Williams but even more indulging are his allegorical ways of bringing realism to the eyes of the reader. You wouldn't know that this is his first book by the free flowing of his words that will leave you exasperated and wanting to go deeper in thought. One thing is for sure, this is the beginning of a vision that not only entails the author but it is intended to serve as a peace offering for mankind with the hopes that each of us might redirect our priorities and recommit ourselves to what matters. It thrives on your wishes to connect with the almighty. And then it leaves you with a question, how much of a role does what you believe in play in your everyday life? Williams, and his dynamic approach leaves us the way he captured our attention by challenging us to personally consider our ways that the magnitude of our understanding may become subjected to a higher power. Awesome.

Katrina C. Williams

Chapter One

The Beginning

I want to talk about things that make up our existence, to discuss some issues relative to each of our "wanna know but never ask" types of questions. I would like to give some insight into the different challenges we face each day relative to the forces of good and evil, which seem to play tug of war with our minds. In this opening chapter, I want to talk about the beginning. You know, before a tree becomes a tree, it is a small seed. Before any offspring are produced, they are small seeds. Before human beings become adults, they are seeds that are nourished and then they become the people we see today. I want to talk about the "before" stage so that what is seen can actually be understood.

Our inquiry here will be one of arriving at a point in time when the source of all things creates a world or should I say all that we see before us today and then "the beginning" is established. We want to discover that as all things have a beginning source, so do we. We want to establish that we are connected to this eternal power because of His own will to begin and complete a work that would forever be subjected to His marvelous power.

The Provider of the Eternal

It is impossible to think of eternal life without first attempting to search for the provider of the eternal itself. In order to understand what eternal is, we have to first accept what it consists of. It has to start with a being greater than we are. We know nothing can first be given unless it is possessed; otherwise it cannot be offered. You cannot sell a car unless you have a car to sell, right? Banks can't offer to loan you money unless they actually have money in house to loan; therefore, our eternal power source has to possess every quality He expects us to have in order to command us to resemble His character.

But before we can know which way is up, we have to look up and put forth the effort required to know such a being, that we might understand the makeup of His character. Our understanding of such a being is critical because without the knowledge of His existence and His operative power in each of our lives, we never realize our potential and we become slaves to the views of society. Therefore, throughout life we learn and form inadequate opinions about others without knowing them for ourselves. We cannot form a just fact or belief about a person when our facts are based upon false assumptions and not personal contact. There is nothing like our own personal encounter with what we seek. Others encourage us by their testimonies but their experiences give us the hope needed to begin our search. Others acknowledging an encounter with a higher source plant the seed, so to speak, but our personal search waters the crop.

Seeds need water to grow just like the natural and spiritual aspects of our character. The better nourished they are, the better chance they have at survival. And just like anything else, the more we feed one side the bigger it grows; the less we feed either side the more feeble it becomes. As any farmer knows, an unwatered crop is useless and eventually becomes plain old soil that has to be retilled. To be retilled means to be reworked, prepared again in order to be useful. Our search has to begin with a prepared foundation in our hearts, ready to believe the experience and capable of accepting the encounter with our beginning source.

To not search for our greater source is to remain in constant need of an encounter, just like our farmer example. Sometimes crops are wiped out and take a long time before the ground is good for planting again. Sometimes drastic things happen in our lives that we might ask the question, "Why?" This can be death, the loss of a job, or even the inability to feel accepted by our peers. But is this the opportunity to allow the feeling of inferiority to rule, or the opportunity to begin a search for a greater source? I don't know, I'm just asking the questions. It's up to you to provide the answers.

So what search are we considering? We are considering a search for the embodiment of our higher source of power. It starts within, and it dwells inside each of us. The catch is that we have to diligently seek for what has already been set aside for us to find.

The Essence of Life

Finding Our Beginning Source

There is a starting point for all things and ours begins with an all-knowing power source. We need to create a relationship with such a power because, as our beginning source, He holds the answers to our personal dilemmas. Getting closer to our beginning source allows us to understand ourselves and our limitations, and more importantly our need for such a being. If we find Him, we find our purpose in life. His discovery does not remove us from the normal temptations and difficulties associated with human life, but we become more confident in our approach to such situations.

Our ancestors' past experiences, which tradition affirms, should not serve as an excuse to resist change or limit the interaction between creation and creator but it should form an eagerness to cling to what controls the future. Racism of the past shouldn't stop African-Americans from loving the Caucasian American or any other American for that matter, and the high levels of hostility because of different cultural backgrounds among nations shouldn't hinder the unification of all people. Rituals should be considered rediscoveries of the past foundations that should be used to build stronger connections with our source of beginning. We should use what others have learned to increase our understanding of our beginning source of power. We should not denounce the new developments of historical facts just because our great-grandmothers and great-grandfathers held different views and experiences.

We have to accept the fact that there are questions to which we as humans have no answers. We have to know that we have a source of power that has lent to us our freedom of choice and His divine image. These foundations need to be the underlying beliefs in a higher power or else we will continue to resist what we should embrace and deny what we should accept. This beginning source becomes a question to mankind because of a search that starts within. Within the depths of our souls we long to know how life began and how it will end. We want to know how did it all start, what makes each of us so different, and what role does society play in its effort to connect with the beginning source of life itself?

Science, believe it or not, does not contradict the being of a greater power. It actually affirms the source of beginning through its factual discoveries. Science cannot give us the security we seek as it pertains to all things. It can only create personal challenges for each of us as individuals to search for our source of beginning by attempting to understand His character. In doing so, we manifest within our lives and ourselves the true identities by which we are known by our creator.

Our beginning source is the answer to all things and it does not matter what denomination we claim to represent or the differences we create amongst ourselves. We are all different of course but we all have a common need, that of a relationship with our source of power. What gives me the right to say we all have a common need, let alone the need of some power source? Well, let me answer a question with a question. We all want peace right? We all want happiness. We all want a life that is fulfilling. To have these things we search for the source of each of these qualities.

Before we are married, we date people with the hope of finding someone who meets every one of our standards and when we find that special someone, we acknowledge before our source and the world that the love bug has landed. Our search for love is also the same strategy we use to search for peace and all the other life-fulfilling qualities we think are necessary for a complete life. To seek for something is to search for the source. When looking for peace, we must find the source of peace. We must find the source of happiness in order to be happy. Some people, who seem to have everything, lack the happiness we think material possessions should bring, and those who seem to have the minimal things in life are the happiest. It is the source that makes the difference.

If we are all to find such a power then we cannot continue to strive against each other, as we are all considered the same, in search of the same things, and in need of the same discoveries. In the beginning source of power, we find unity. Resist that discovery, we maintain what we have—a world in chaos.

Knowing Him Through Experience

Though opinions differ and views change, the true perspective of life only leads to one being. As much as most of us would like to reserve our right for spiritual interaction as a sort of private mission, it is really the essence of what life is all about. The beginning is the focal point, where nothing becomes something and where matter becomes energy and where darkness becomes light. We all wish for the foreknowledge of beginnings so that we might know the end in its entirety, and so that we might find a way not to lose what we feel we have. What do we have? Most of us fear the loss of control. We acknowledge the existence of a greater being but fail to demonstrate what we proclaim because we would have to become subject to what we believe. For many of us this is not easy because we are faced with a society that teaches us to take control of our lives, surrendering to none. We are placed in an awkward position because we strongly believe in what's right but we risk walking alone in order to be correct. So what we have, we wish to keep and that's control—from the life we choose to live to where we choose to live and what we choose to believe in. We find ourselves in the middle of the street. One side has its limitations but at least the outcome can be seen. The other side requires trust, sacrifice, and belief, qualities we know to exist but that are not visible. With one lies the destiny we consider our dream and with the other, a destiny only found by seeking such a beginning source.

But in order to find and connect with such a beginning source, we have to digest Him as we gain knowledge through our natural course of maturity. As children we learn to understand the sounds of different words and then we learn the words. We watch by observation before we realize what the uses of our body members are. Babies watch their parents or siblings before realizing they have hands and fingers, feet and toes that work the same way. With that attained knowledge we begin to crawl and then to walk. It takes time but it all starts with the first step, the beginning.

Teenagers while developing their own standards and values are influenced by what they experience in their homes. If they never witness persistence and perseverance, then neither will they diligently seek for Him who holds the keys of life. Education is understood by the same principles. We learn at one level and then we move to the next level until we have completed the requirements that allow us to be considered learned or educated.

But it all starts with a beginning. After we are considered adults, we move to another phase of life termed independence. We now work, provide, and feed ourselves, no longer expecting or relying on anyone else to do it. We are what our maturity commands us to be, responsible people free to choose, but not with the right to refuse what will never cease to exist—our beginning source. This level of maturity not only allows us to make up our own minds but it causes a burning incompleteness that desires to be filled.

The problem is that no one can fill this void. Sure there are temporary substitutes but none ever take the place of such an empty hole that needs to be filled.

This hole is a craving each of us has, be it consciously or subconsciously. It is the search for our beginning source of power. All the survival techniques involved in facing life and its issues stem from this beginning source of power. So in essence, we as human beings have no need to commit suicide or inflict pain upon ourselves for things we have no control over. Instead we should seek the power that has the answers to help us maintain our self-control so that we do not lose before we have an opportunity to win.

The Beginning Holds the Answers

In order to trust and understand this beginning source, we have to believe in our hearts that the initial setup of life began with one all-powerful and infinite being. To believe this is to recognize that the natural things are only revealed by one source. This source of power is our reference point as to what is possible and what isn't. It defines our limitations as human beings and exposes our weaknesses as created people.

To search for this power is to respond to our personal dilemmas. For who else better to deal with our issues than the creator of our souls. We all have the right to believe in other theories even if they oppose the truth; however, we cannot dismiss the fact that the creator of our minds is worthy of our acknowledgment as the supreme ruler of our souls.

Because we are created beings in the image of the greatest being, we are granted the right to make decisions for ourselves that will affect our lives and those around us. We term this right *free will*. But free will should not be taken lightly as if our decisions can alter the course of life. Our decisions can prolong or interrupt our designed purpose, causing us to miss out on any obstacles we should conquer and any success we should experience. But it cannot change the mind of our creator, although it can affect our pathway to Him. After all, free will is a characteristic of the greatest being since the beginning of time and as we were made in His image, we too were given this dangerous aspect of life. It is dangerous because with it we can deny the creator of our lives.

We can develop reasons to justify our own shortcomings that become excuses for not acknowledging this beginning source of power. This power source moves mankind to study His creation and to ponder His next moves, never to be completely sure of how He does what He does. Mankind wants to know its beginning source. This is seen in the constant innovation of technology through different and better modes of communication. Man is trying to become independent of his creator so that at the push of a button his every desire can be satisfied. But there is still something that won't let go of his soul—the beginning. Man wasn't there and now to understand it he must search for the beginning source within himself.

In all that man seeks to do, nothing moves or motivates him more than to be close to the discovery of life. He awakes everyday with the same inquisitive spirit that he went to sleep with. He wants to know what makes people different and why the differences of mentalities exist. How can part of creation love and embrace and, at the same time, the other hate and divide. He wants to find out how he was perfectly made and chemically united with the forces of the universe. He wants to know how he can control his body weight and work with gravity in such a way that he doesn't just float away. He is looking for the beginning because it holds all the answers and it is the only source that can make him feel whole again. I said *again* because we only seek to find something that we had before. If we never had it we never miss it and we never realize we need it. But because of some feeling of connection of which each living soul has, we all in our own way seek to find our true place, our beginning.

Substitutes for Our Source

Some of us seek to satisfy our soul by idol worship, meaning we have selective interest that occupies more of our time than our search for the beginning does. We become more interested in wealth than contentment. We become more concerned with what people think of us instead of what we make people think of us. Materially, we become attached to things as an expression of accomplishment. We begin to want those things more than we want our source. Some people continue in age-old rituals that do more destroying of the soul than the discovering of it. Many remain embedded in traditional views without ever really knowing why, only that it requires no commitment but just acceptance. Some of us even join cults. It is all an attempt to unite with the power source from the beginning. We are looking for a reason to trust and believe.

I say we because although the world population just surpassed five billion, we are all still united souls as long as what one does affects the others. We all have the right to make choices because of the image in which we were created. But none of us has the right to substitute, reject, or deny the existence of such a great power. This great source obviously made a choice to bring forth mankind without being forced to from another being. Therefore He gave us the same choice, not one of creating a world, but the opportunity to choose. We are all different because of the decisions we make and the preferences we have, but as far as the beginning goes, we were all given the necessary tools to make the proper decisions. This is what mankind has in common with each other—the image of its beginning source.

The Beginning

We also have to understand that, with the search for our beginning, we all deal with obstacles which serve as deceptions and walls between us and our finding our original source. Just as we cannot have a cause without a force, or an effect without a cause, we cannot have a future without a beginning. How we cultivate a relationship with such a source determines the type of confidence in the future we will have. We may not wish to admit it, but our destinies are dependent upon one source, our beginning source of power. Is it possible that the beginning lives in each of us and that the only way to find it is to search what it occupies? Could such a great creator have equipped His creation with a tracking device? A type of device that could take in as well as distribute. One that could communicate with its creator anytime it wanted to. Could this creator have established a centerpiece that would form the foundation upon which its actions would be weighed? Is there any greater mode of emotional expression or divine connection than that of the heart?

Man Contains What He Seeks

The heart of man is his source of life but it is also his mode of reception from his beginning source. Can a man actually contain what he seeks? This would have to be the case if we were made in the image of this almighty being. We contain a part of eternity. What is created cannot be more than its creator; therefore, what is created contains part of the substance of which it was made. Whether what is created chooses to acknowledge the source of its substance doesn't change the fact that it still remains a part of it. And now the truth is revealed through what was made and the dictations of the heart determine each of our actions.

In this stage of differentiating between the imagined and the revealed, we have a close encounter with our beginning source. It usually happens through a small powerful voice that just won't stop repeating itself. We usually describe this feeling or force as a gut feeling, a voice that continues to challenge our natural will with that of a higher realm. This voice is the same voice that gave us a choice—the same voice that we seek to know and to find and to hear constantly. It is our confirmation. It is our source. When we hear this voice, it isn't a sound so common to the ear or the mind. In fact, we could say that it is an out-of-the-mind experience, but in one thing rest assured—when we hear this voice we have found what we've been looking for, our beginning.

It is in the beginning that we receive instructions and directions as to which moves to make. It is from the source of the beginning that we have our existence. Agree or disagree, we cannot operate alone or we would self-destruct. The pathway of humankind is limited. If left to determine our own way, we would never have peace of mind or rest to the soul because the appetite through the human eyes is never full. It seeks to consume and fulfill its desires everyday. Seeking his beginning source causes mankind to resist what he would naturally accept, relative to his natural instincts.

For example, our natural response when a married woman or married man makes a pass at us, especially if no one is looking, is to inadvertently flirt. This is not to say that we do, it is just to emphasize our normal reaction to common desires. What about that wallet that was stolen but never reported, remaining in our hands? Is it out of sight and out of mind, or should our natural responses be tried by something greater? The common temptations that are so natural but so detrimental to our souls are stepping-stones, because our decisions reflect our connection to a greater source.

What a dilemma! Each of us needs such a connection so that our lives will not become meaningless but will reflect the image of our source. We do not know all that we wish to know but we know all that we need to know. Therefore, we are without excuse when it comes to seeking our source of power with all of our heart. We have no reason to dwell in this life without using the power we have been given as by-products of the image in which we were created.

Parental Provision and Protection

Our beginning source paints the picture for us, which can be understood in the example of a father and a son. The father was before the son and the son can only trace his roots to his father. The son learns from the father and the father teaches the son. The son may ask questions pertaining to the thoughts of the father before he was conceived; however, the son never completely understands the courses of action because he wasn't there. It becomes enough for him to trust in the father's words and to believe his father.

It sounds strange but could our source be relaying a message to His creation through our parental guides? I should say so if the parents are examples for their children in provision and in protection. As parents demonstrate to their children the correct way to act, speak, and live, so does our power source, by the way He injects Himself into our lives when we least expect it. We call it intuition, but He calls it parental provision and protection.

Think about it—our parents are the reflections of their own instructions. They are the end result of what our personhood should consist of. Just as we reflect the image of our human parents, we too possess the image of our original creator. Reflecting an image involves projecting a role. As children, our parents teach us and discipline us that we might understand obedience and respect. As a result we teach our children the same things and so on and so forth.

In committing ourselves to such actions we magnify a role, which society confuses with fame and success. We magnify such a role because we become guides, teachers, and instructors of the right way. But more importantly we become the reflection of what our original source meant for us to be. Society calls it being a role model. Human beings call it consideration and respect. But our source of power calls it reflecting the divine image of our creator.

Too often we allow society to make us believe we have to follow and believe the words of those whose pockets are as deep as the ocean and whose face is universally known. The error in such vain manipulation is that we are forced to follow something we will never catch, and to listen to someone we will never know. How can such people be considered role models? Don't get me wrong, the highly successful should be model citizens in how they conduct themselves, and they should be examples to those of us who seek to achieve. But by no means should they be considered role models because they cannot be such. A role model is just that, someone who plays a role constantly, meaning every day. They lead, they guide, they listen, they instruct, and they disagree with us when we stray away from the truth. Parents are the only real role models. They allow us to reflect our true role model, our beginning source of life. Could parenthood be a divine position as it relates to our source? Of course it is. Through it we see the ultimate goal of respect, subjection, and obedience. We are the offspring of a mighty source of power and we demonstrate our response to such power by our responses to our parents and to each other.

The Foundation of Success

Our beginning source looks for us daily by manifesting Himself through many modes of communication, and to

The Beginning

resist Him is to ignore Him. This is a form of distrust, not believing that the source of all power is able to communicate with what He has made. Now let's speak plainly. As a father or a mother, you instruct your child to come home after school and to go inside the house and start dinner. But before all that you specifically remind him or her to call you at work to let you know they made it home and everything is fine. The child doesn't know it but you already told the next-door neighbor to look out at a specific hour to make sure that everything goes well with your child, as you are trying to gradually lengthen the rope of supervision. The child, knowing the hour of your usual arrival home after work, doesn't come straight home but goes over to a friends house aware of the fact that he or she has a few hours to spare before you arrive home. After engaging in other activities, the child finally goes home. Arriving home, he or she is exhausted and falls down on the couch asleep even forgetting to make dinner as instructed. When you, as a parent, arrive the child acts as if he or she has been there all the time and because of a busy school day, was tired and dozed off to sleep. One phone call to the good neighbor answers the question of whether the child can be trusted to obey the rules. It isn't that going over to a friend's house was a bad thing. It just wasn't what was specifically told to the child. Although there will be many other opportunities for the child to gain your trust, the next time the child is given particular instructions to carry out a task, he or she is going to have to prove worthy of your trust before you, without any reservations, trust them. This is not to say that the expected bad will continue to come out of the intended good. It just means that along the instructional lines, a wrong decision was made and consequences have to be suffered in order for the child's steps to be ordered. This is an important example because obedience is the foundation of success.

Think about it. Obedience determines how committed we will be to the goals we wish to achieve, because to fulfill our dreams we have to submit or obey certain precepts as they relate to our dream. It determines our determination to achieve because after we see that what we imagined won't be as easy as we thought, we may lose our motivation. Obedience also determines the value we place upon what is considered important in life. It could be our family, our job, and even our God. Our faith in our God is affected by our obedience. We cannot seek the beginning source without being willing to obey and follow the precepts He commands. Since we as human beings are finite beings, our time clock keeps ticking, not leaving much room for disobedient behaviors.

This takes us back to the beginning, to realize that our creator makes us and then walks with us. He never leaves us and He always gives us another chance. How, we ask? If you're reading this book then obviously some good source thought it good to wake you up this day that you might ask Him a question or two that He might speak for Himself directly to you. Because He is the creator of time, He is not subjected to it nor is He limited by it. But we are, and no matter how many chances He gives us, our time is running out. So with all the questions as to our existence and the beginning of time, we see that it all starts with the only true power.

If we look beyond what is staring us in the face to other sources for explanations, we become sorcerers, witchcraft believers, and not patient followers of the only true power who has promised to reveal Himself in an appointed time. Naturally, we as humans have questions about things which even the angels desire to investigate, but we cannot allow our minds to trick us or to cause us to not remain patient in our expectations.

We also must remember that our minds serve as the CPUs of our existence and are the main battlefield for our outlook and our influences. So it's safe to say that our outlook and influences are affected by the choices we make, pertaining to our free will. Each of us are different because we are affected by different things at different times in different ways. We are not all carpenters. Nor are we all electricians, but we have a number of differences among us that we might not lack the necessary capability to be self-sufficient. All of these characteristics point to an abiding source of power that first demonstrated such independence and control. To deny such a beginning source the title of the reigning King is to allow the opposite force of His character to live in what our creator should possess—our minds.

We have to agree that there are opposing forces to the truth just as there are truths that oppose negative forces. This is not something that needs to be argued but can be understood in our own personal knowledge of good and evil. For example, we know in our mind and our heart that to curse someone is not a good thing to do, even if they cursed us first. Something inside tells us that cursing is a bad thing to do. Could this stem from the beginning good in whose image we were created? It all stems from the beginning image of this almighty being because none of us naturally knows how to perform what is good and neither did we know before it was first revealed to us. Therefore, to have to make choices is a challenging stage that seeks to prove what we claim to believe in.

Our Opportunity to Choose

Indeed, this great being created mankind because He wanted to. There is not a sign of any greater force that pulled his arm or his leg, to determine what He would and should create. He gave us the opportunity to choose against what He represented in order to maintain the openness involved in a relationship. He advises us against opposing His power or existence by the consequences we face in doing so.

An electrical contractor can wire a house any way he chooses as long as it meets the inspector's wishes and passes the codes. To do it any other way would not be advisable nor acceptable because of the ramifications involved and the risk that could cause death. In the same way this almighty being says we are free to do as we please but any decision made without His acceptance could possibly be harmful to us. Society tells us we live in a democracy, free to do what we wish as often as we wish, but we are not completely free of our original source. We should seek to know these things so that we can avoid all the unnecessary obstacles involved in trying to replace the irreplaceable.

Anytime we try to substitute or create our own source of power or even explain our well-thought-out logic, we must understand that we are allowing the negative forces to intrude and influence our minds, causing us to distance ourselves from our source. The opposing forces make us think we are different because of our position in society or our income bracket. These forces seek to divide and conquer. These forces wish to change the way we search for our beginning power. A little distraction can cause many of us to abort the ship and watch it sink not knowing we have the power to keep it afloat.

Could our creator really love His creation, having allowed such a dilemma? Could this force be demonstrating to us, by us, among us, the meaning and direction we should be receiving from Him? I do not mean to pose questions without answers but these are personal issues and dilemmas, which serve to our individual benefit if we individually answer them. Who knows, maybe we could all find our beginning and the power source by which we live and the faith necessary to believe there is a creator who loves us all as one people, who sees no color or status position but only an opportunity to reveal Himself to His creation if they will accept Him. I say *if they will accept Him* because once again we have that choice to make and, no matter what the choice is, there is a benefit or a consequence to face.

I do not wish to theologically debate the issues of the substance of God or Jesus Christ. I do not think it is time to do that here. These are what I feel to be inspired words as it pertains to our beginning source of life, God.

Chapter Two

Deception

It is breathtaking sometimes how magicians can make us believe we see things that we do not see or objects floating in front of our eyes—objects that are really immovable. They make us see or think things that do not exist. We in turn choose to describe these types of acts as magic and the persons as masters of deception.

Just as there are good forces and bad forces, evil spirits and good spirits, could the CPU of our existence, our minds, be affected by forces which contradict the truth, leading us to make decisions based on deception? If our intended purpose was perfection but a wrong choice led to deception then we are agreeing that a negative force interrupted our original perfect state, right?

Therefore, the battlefield of our existence, our minds, is affected or infected by what it chooses to receive. Yes, what it chooses to receive or what we allow ourselves to receive. We all know that we can become products of our environment if we choose to. We also know that our direct associations and interactions with people can affect us in one way or another. These influences are the results of the choices we make. Our own common sense gives us the comfort we seek and it speaks to us from time to time, causing us to weigh the options of the choices we have to make.

The extent of the influence depends on us and which forces we allow to manifest themselves through our minds. We become winners because we believe in our minds that we are, and we will not accept anything less. Not realizing our potential is due to the fact that we compromise our integrity and our will in our minds. Either way, our realizations materialize based solely on the fact of which forces we allow to enlighten us or deceive us.

Opposing Forces

If there is a positive force which generates happiness, joy, and love then there is another force which generates unhappiness, sadness, and hate. These are not equal and opposing forces because that would make our power source a hypocrite and a contradictor, which we know to be impossible. Let me explain it this way. This creator could not say one thing and then do another. He could not make us in such a powerful image to represent the good if He also represented the bad. He would constantly be in conflict with Himself and we would have no reason to look for Him because He couldn't exist in this way. Any force that is in direct contradiction with itself eventually fades away. Hot water mixed with cold water becomes warm water. It is neither hot nor cold and doesn't serve the purpose for either. Therefore, He could never call us bad if He made us bad.

But because free will was challenged by deception and infected mankind, we have our own differences of beliefs and understandings about what power means and from where it comes. We even argue about our own existence and our beginning source. So throughout the course of history we have developed different denominations for our own comfort. We have watched the formation of cultic groups that seek to monopolize mankind, leading them away from what they claim to seek. Indeed, we are all different with different mentalities as well as characteristics of interest, but one thing that we all have in common is our beginning source, which wants to expose deceptive forces attempting to tangle us in a web of confusion.

The Creator of Right

Deception is a way to make us believe something that isn't true. The more we see it the more we believe it, even though it really doesn't exist. Yes, it's a mind game and the master of deception is he who has opposed the truth from the beginning. What is the truth, we often ask? The truth is what we know to be right. It doesn't matter where right came from but that we know it exists. Tracing it back to the beginning we find out what we already knew—that our power source is greater than we are, and right can only be what the creator of right has made it to be. Our intuition tells us what right is.

The problem begins when we logically try to find or explain right. This almighty being cannot be understood in the logical realm because our minds are finite and can only deal with things that make sense to us. Therefore, to try to make a limitless power source limited or explainable is an attempt to define his character. To attempt to define a force that can't be defined is to restrict its power.

But deception can make us think that this power source doesn't really exist because if it did, then why is life so difficult and happiness so hard to find? Why are criminal acts committed each day and why are some countries more powerful, while others cannot even feed their population. Why do babies die and who ever created the marijuana plant? If we ever knew why, would we ever understand? Is life so difficult because many of us choose to put off right choices, making unhappiness a consequence rather than a predestinated place? Is happiness far from each of us or are we deceived into thinking that certain things only happen to certain people? Is happiness really that hard to find or do many of us want to find it in our own way?

To find happiness requires sacrifice. It requires knowledge of recognizing what matters and what doesn't. Our happiness is independent of everyone else's happiness but it requires the use of the same force in order to find it. It cannot depend on our possessions because we possess different things every day. Happiness is not a conditional trait. It is a positive characteristic from a positive force. It is found by those who unconditionally embrace it through the good times and the bad and who seek to fulfill it by allowing the source of happiness to dwell within their soul.

This is why we see people who from a material standpoint seem to have nothing but are the happiest people we could ever meet. They have embraced happiness and they won't let it go. More importantly, they have allowed the source of happiness to dwell within their soul. We can also testify to the fact that there are some who materially possess all that there is but can't sleep at night because happiness is far from them. Their happiness depends on what they possess and, even, worse they have not allowed the source of happiness to dwell in their souls. They replace Him with what they can possess and therefore always have conditional happiness.

Crimes, which are committed daily—are they the results of human choices which do render just consequences? Our backgrounds are different, and our upbringings and influences are completely different. Some of us grew up with a silver spoon in our mouths and some of us grew up without a spoon at all. Could it be negative influences from truth-opposing forces that only stem from deception? Of course some force dictates every action whether it's good or bad. But either way crime is the result of a bad choice by a bad force, a deceptive force which makes us think there is no other way. It seeks to oppose the known good that is part of our original characteristic. It wants to magnify our weaknesses and shortcomings so that our choices become limited and our power non-existent. This is the grand purpose of deception.

To magnify the negatives overrules the positives and causes us to act like a kid on Halloween dressed in a costume, covering up our true identity. The difference is, the kid at the end of the evening removes the costume and reclaims his original identity, whereas some people live all of their lives dressed in a costume. They are no different than we are but deception has them locked away in the unknown. Who knows, maybe a positive word from someone following a positive source can reunite them with their beginning source, alter their life, and save a soul.

Are some countries more powerful because they embrace the truth of existence even in the midst of its shortcomings as a human race? People make up the whole world. They are the fine pieces that make the world what it is. Some countries have adopted their own definition of the only true source of power. They have defined the beginning and the end of life within their own comfort zones of understanding. Deceiving some and challenging others, either way their voice is spoken and prosperity or lack thereof is a result of those proclamations. Although there are no perfect countries, in which every deed is just or correct, there are those which attempt to follow that which is historically proven and not traditionally justified, who do reap the fruits of their labor.

The debatable issue is that of death. Should we blame our creator for the expiration of human time or accept His actions as one who is always in control? I think we should accept the fact that one supreme being rules and reigns. It will be His way or no way. Pain from the disappearance of loved ones causes us to question, but the ability to recognize our power source causes us to surrender.

Deception makes us think we should live forever without adhering to any rules. It makes us think the creative force owes us an explanation when the timetable of life says time is up. There is a constant struggle between what we feel is acceptable and what actually happens. But death isn't a bad thing—it is a necessary thing. It is an opportunity to move from one realm to another. To a certain degree, death is like a bridge; you need it to get from one side to the other. As our bodies get older and our eyesight dwindles, it is only natural that death is inevitable. It's not the act of passing away that is so bad; it is the fear of not knowing where we pass to. This is where deception becomes stronger and leads us away from what we should be growing closer to. To know our source of power doesn't mean we will understand all things but it does give us the ability to deal with whatever comes our way, even death.

Drugs and other inventions which serve as harmful utensils that give us a false sense of fun—should we blame the misuse of such things on the Almighty or accept that we have just as much right to deny them as use them. It is our choice and to blame anyone for our decisions is to allow deception to rule.

These answers may not be acceptable because they require each of us to depend on something not every one of us has—faith. Faith in what, you might ask? Faith in the force that created us and that is greater than we are.

Division Distracts from the Creator

Deception makes us forget our source of power. And anything that is forgotten is not used. If we had power but never used it, we would become susceptible to any force that catered to our interest. Yes, if we were made in the image of a perfect being and were deceived, and in a sense demoted, we would need our power source in order to be promoted back to our previous position. Deception tries to prevent us from seeking this power. How does deception do that? Let's look at an example which has affected the whole world and still does.

Racism. Is racism a learned act or a deception? Indeed, generations seems to pass down, with their history, certain stereotypes related to groups and customs. Current statistical data reveals racial profiling—the notion that most African Americans are thought to be more aggressive criminals than any other race. And then there is the intelligence factor. Is there equal opportunity? You be the judge. I could offer an unlimited amount of statistical information but that would do nothing but persuade you to agree with my opinion. But question yourself and let the inner truth that wishes to be heard speak by what you believe and not by what you are persuaded to believe. Persuasion is a strong force and our role models help to free us from the bonds of discrimination or they help us remain in the segregated thoughts of the past.

Parents play a role in what their children learn and understand and how they perceive interactions with everyone.

The Essence of Life

So of course, what one is taught at home affects and influences the outlook of the person. But could this be a generational deception meant to maintain a division amongst the people, so that a unified belief and acceptance of one Supreme Being could not take place? Does this force use human differences and preferences to justify its intentions to influence us? Yes it does, as long as one race continues to think in terms of its superiority to the others. The purpose of this particular deception is to distract us from focusing and seeking the knowledge of our creator. It affects all races and all cultures and maintains a division that we may focus more on our own issues instead of allowing our creator to intervene.

Deception is a trick of the mind. It's like magic. It wants us to magnify our small issues that they may seem to rule the world, and belittle the positive things that we may not become addicted to such. Although we all have differences, they shouldn't be a reason to maintain a division between us as people. Could there be something trying to keep us from finding our source of power? That voice inside which tells us we cannot do something, or that we're not good enough for the aspirations we have or the dreams we chase, could we be in the midst of a crossroad between the fulfilling of a mission and the acceptance of a deception?

Deception seeks to consume us and close our minds so that what is true and simple will always be questioned and not received. It acts as a maze in each of our lives. Instead of believing the life and power that exist in each of us, we travel through life being affected by turns and paths, which we could completely avoid if we only realized the use of deception. Should we all think only good things? I do not know if that is possible, given the human nature, but I would say we all can know the difference between our various thoughts and which ones we should act upon.

The Distortion of Deception

We are all presented with different challenges by different thoughts and it is exonerating to be able to explain each because it gives us a sense of knowledge. Our actions, however, define our thoughts and the consequence of our actions justifies or defends our thoughts whether good or bad. The deception is seen when we try to justify what we know to be wrong although our situation tells us it's right. We have to understand that having the right to do something does not make it right. Because we are inherently good beings, we know how to differentiate in implementing our thoughts. Deception tries to intervene in the implementation stage because if what is projected or expected can be changed or questioned, our confidence in the power granted to us to bring to pass all that we think is limited.

This in turn stops the seeking process. The seeking process is made up of goal-seeking, fantasy-dreaming, and aspiration-seeking. If we realize our goal or aspiration, we find a part of our beginning, which gives us peace and a sense of accomplishment. The negative forces, which try to intervene to limit our accomplishments, show up in the form of deception so that the peace we seek, we can't find, and the overall satisfaction with the good in life, we never believe. Spiritually, we define this deception as sin. In human terms we explain it as being confused. And those in the middle say it is a form of bad luck.

Deception is tricky in that it wants us to think things that do not exist, but yet are real. I must explain myself here so that my words are not seen as contradictory. Anything that is perceived is real. But everything perceived is not meant to become reality. The magicians distort the truth to make us think we see something they merely created. It never changes what exists—it just makes us think what exists is not what we see.

The Essence of Life

Now if the intended good from our original superior power was meant for our recognition of any force to the contrary, then we as humankind do in fact rule over any force which tries to intervene. Simply stated, deception has only as much power as we give it. It can only operate if we allow it to. I do not believe that a rabbit comes out of a hat. But if I ponder the possibilities relative to the actions of the magicians, sooner or later I will accept that it is possible. The truth or deception. Now we know the answer to this question. We know rabbits do not come out of hats but magicians sure make it look possible. We are all made in the image of our creator in that we have a mind, a heart, and a soul. We are spiritual beings as well as human beings. This statement is even true for those who deny their creator. To deny one part doesn't mean the other doesn't exist, but means we choose to receive and accept one part and deny the other. The rabbit in the hat is believed to be true after we see the appearance of the rabbit from what appears to be thin air. The deception takes place in making something seem real that never did exist.

Our lives as individuals encounter all types of situations where the truth is constantly tested by the force of deception. Think about it. Why do some people have a never-give-up spirit and others fold at the sign of trouble? Could the force of deception limit their self-confidence, which would limit their outlook, causing fear? Some people overcome such a force by choosing the greater force, which secures their confidence and empowers their self-esteem, while others neglect the good source and are discouraged rather than encouraged.

Why are some families stricken with generational curses, which seem to keep inflicting the same temptations or challenges. The deceptive force chooses the mode to intervene by which it has been the most successful. If I'm right, and I think I am, have you wondered why some families are smokers? Not just one or two people in the family, but everyone smokes. Perform a background check and you'll find that their grandparents smoked and now the torch literally is passed on to the next generation. I use smoking as an example because we all know it is not good for us. And unless you have stopped reading this book, you are discovering that anything not good for us is a deception and deception weeds its way into our lives any way we let it. Wherever our weak links are, that is the target point for intrusion. It's difficult to change the course of the generational temptation. Is this an excuse to resist change or a reason not to change? You make the call. After all, your life and your children's generation depend on the choices you make. This force is not prejudiced and it acts as a sort of blob that grows relative to its consumption. This force is not just after us personally but it wants to affect everything we associate with—our families and friends and anything else we hold close to heart.

Deception Is Oppression

A problem is always a problem until it is exposed or confronted. A problem left to linger around is like a tornado, which takes force and speed over time and eventually becomes out of control, damaging everything in its path. Deception is like this. It is a problem which, if not recognized, affects every area of our thinking, and then it attacks our self-esteem, which is the foundation of our confidence. This is where we become the little engine that could but not the little engine that would. Some people choose to overcome because of a force they believe in, which exists deep in the soul. When challenged with the deception that brings doubt and discouragement, this part of the soul pays more attention to the positive power source and chooses to listen to the inner voice, its source. From a human standpoint we may prefer to engage in discrepancies proposed by other theorists relative to the mind and how it works. The role which deception plays, however, explains all the shortcomings where human knowledge fails.

Deception is not so much depression as oppression. It weighs us down and causes us to look more at the cons instead of the pros. Indeed the cons have to play a part in the final decision but it must be understood as to the type of force it is trying to institute. We agree that anything negative does not stem from the good but from a force that opposes the good, right? Therefore, deception can always be exposed because it intends to deceive. It has a goal or a contract on our life just as the good forces do. The height of success is measured by the effects of the encounters with good and bad forces and to what extent we give control to either force.

Now we know that life stems from a good source, because it is a good thing. I cannot imagine success or aspirations in the mind of the dead, so we can agree that this being who decided to give life actually had life to give. Therefore, it was His choice to share what He already had. This makes Him good if we interpret good as doing something we are not required to do. No one pulls our arm or casts us into prison if we choose not to speak to someone who speaks to us, but because it seems fitting and respectful, we cordially respond in an acceptable manner. Whether we term it obligation or willingness, it stems from the good that is inside, a characteristic which comes from our creator.

Deception does not come from the good because the good source does not need to confuse or deceive Himself. His creation or offspring would never be obligated to seek the meaning of life through Him if He would give us life and then plant the seed to destroy it. His creation would be useless. But if forces opposed to the truth from the beginning could never face the truth in a one-on-one match to decide who is the king, then it would make sense for the opposing forces to try to intercept the goal of the creator through what He created. One word—*deception*. The greatest trick the opposing forces ever pulled was trying to convince the world that their creator never existed. This is a spiritual attack upon your soul. Those who give attention to their inner man, their inner soul, their spirit man, are the ones who recognize the opposing forces and are able to overcome what used to keep them down. Those who continue to struggle and make the same mistakes, by either blaming others or refusing to keep an open mind relative to the issues of life, are the ones who never get out of this life all that their creator meant for them to.

The Mind Determines What We Receive

This game of deception tries our mind before our heart because our mind is an avenue to our heart. In our mind we choose to believe deception or to dismiss it, not allowing it to enter into our heart. Out of the heart come the issues of life but not before they're tried in the mind. We believe in God because of an encounter in the mind. Our heart is changed by what the mind determines to receive. The subconscious is the truth of the soul and this is where the interaction takes place. The curiosities of life are here. There are secrets here that we suppress, hoping that we can forget them, but this spiritual interaction commands the revelation of all things. To accept Him here, in our subconscious, is to change our life and to coincide with what was preordained for our souls. To deny Him is to accept condemnation and belief in the fact that our life is sufficiently good and in need of no change. Does God really love what He created to allow such a dilemma? Before we answer this question let me ask you a question. Is deception an accusation embedded in mankind as a sign of its shortcomings? Or is it an obstacle, designed to eliminate the truth, coming between us and our source of power?

Many of us will endure enormous amounts of pain, struggle, and self-belittlement to achieve a position of quality and importance. We will compromise our faith and our beliefs for a shot at the big time. It may take us years to climb the ladder of selfishness only to find that it takes less than an hour to be returned to a starting position. Our desire for accomplishment at all costs paves the way for our disappointments. Could deception have made us think that we could stand alone? After all, we determine our own destiny, right? We are in control. We sweat and lose sleep and therefore, when our time of reward is granted, we feel more than deserving because we put in the time and we are what we achieve. This deceptive spirit wants us to think this way. It wants us to believe in ourselves because if we believe in a higher source of power we might just achieve all that we set out to achieve. Don't be deceived, our higher source of power is not mocked. To depend on our own strength is to not only be deceived but to set the stage for our own downfall.

Now getting back to the question, does God really love what He created to have allowed such a dilemma? I'm only writing what I feel to be inspired words from our beginning source, God, and it's time for the deceiver to be recognized and exposed. Those who want to withstand the test of time will do so as it pertains to prosperity, love, knowledge, and the good which each of us was created to do. So the answer to the question is yes, God did love what He created so much that He gave us a choice. What a power source, what a God!

Chapter Three

Reality

Why is reality so hard for most of us to face? I am sure it has to do with the fact that the truth unveils what we choose to hide or suppress. Who is this truth which does such a thing? We will get to this in a bit, but stay with me here and let's see if we can recognize what reality really is. So far we know that whether we individually acknowledge that we have a beginning source or not, it still exists. Even if we choose to continue to try to explain something that cannot be explained, His purpose never changes for what He created. He will always be what He is—God, the only true power source there ever was and the only power source there ever will be. Reality is the recognition of a realization of what is true. It's an acknowledgment of a higher good in its purest form.

When we fall in love we have a tendency to lose touch with reality, so to speak. We forget to eat, we smile at everything the other person does, and we have a tendency to hold them above every standard we previously set for ourselves, all because they touched a part of our most intimate source of existence, our heart. After some time and a few steps below the love-filled clouds, we find ourselves looking at that person as a regular person, not that we like or love them any less, but the truth has revealed a human being with limitations, one incapable of consistently being all that we imagined. I say consistently because they are everything to us for some time but, over the course of time, the truth reveals what makes that person tick and now we see the person behind the face; we see the truth. Strange how life works but it's even stranger how reality reveals the working of life.

As man is a two-fold being, meaning he is both spiritual and carnal, his greatest achievements and satisfactions are realized when he faces reality. Reality is seeing what the truth reveals. It is connected to our spiritual side because it's the truth, whereas our carnal side or our natural side is what human instincts reveal. We as human beings choose not to see the truth for selfish reasons. We would rather avoid the truth because the truth makes us decide between what's real and what we wish for. Reality constantly tries our beliefs. Our source of power uses reality, which is a characteristic of His personhood, so that we never forget Him.

It's nice to think that we create our own opportunities and to a certain degree we do; however, that degree is dependent upon how close we walk with reality. When I say *walk* I mean how we accept and implement what we know to be real. It is not that most of us don't believe in the existence or intervention of a higher power; we just don't implement the truth of that revelation in our lives. We don't walk it like we talk it.

Anytime there is a struggle with how to believe what's right and how to justify what's wrong, we are in a state of confusion and our human instincts step to the plate. Our minds begin to play tricks on us. We are never in complete darkness regarding the consequences of our decisions; we just are willing to justify an understood wrong instead of believe in a proven right. What is this proven right? The proven right is one that can justify itself and needs no logistics to be completely understood. The proven right is that part of our human makeup that resembles the image in which we were created. The proven right is your spiritual connection with your real source of power.

Reality is humankind's strength. It reverses his path when he deviates from it. It stands in front of him when he wishes to justify his deeds. It picks him up when he settles for less than he should. Reality instructs our focus. It buries our standards and values in what should be our source anyway, our higher power. No matter the culture or race or denomination, reality controls history. It rules because it's real. For it to be real it has to be a characteristic of the ultimate power source.

The purpose was so that man could never be sure by himself, but indirectly would use a part of his creator even if he chose not to acknowledge His existence. So the truth is, whether we as people decide to believe and trust in our maker or not, we still in some way utilize His existence by the very things we believe. We often use the expression, lets face reality. What are we really saying? We are really saying, *let's get in tune with our spiritual side that we might connect with the truth and find our pathway toward the everlasting.*

To See Reality Is to See Our Maker

Now the question is raised as to the order of creation. Was the spiritual side created first or the natural human side? If our source of power decided to make a people for Himself who from the beginning of time could do no wrong, that would make what He created like Him—perfect. As long as what He created trusted in its source of power, he had no decision problems. As long as reality kept him under control relative to his source, perfection was his and destruction would have to wait. Therefore since the source of power is all good and spiritually divine, then we as His offspring were first made spiritual beings, giving us a conception of reality and knowing how to find it when necessary.

We never became out of touch with reality, our true existence, until we deviate from the truth. When our own minds begin to work and make decisions for ourselves, influence of many forms causes us to become infected by things which never should affect us. So we see that our true side was a common side created first for our good as it related to our power source and then as it related to our course of life.

Reality was and is our guide but confusion and wrong choices take place when we choose not to face reality. This causes us to fold under pressure because we forget the very image in which we were created. Reality is true and real and has power from the source of power to give us strength in the time of need. We neglect our power source when the deception or shortcoming causes us to forget it. In order to regain direction and purpose we have to face reality. We have to go back and search our souls for what we know to be there, removing the smoke screen from our eyes, so that we can see the good intentions of creation, and rise and walk again.

So we see as the truth reveals itself we find it to be our measuring tool for all of our affairs. Think about it—we all would like honesty to rule the world in which we live. We all would like our spouses to be completely honest with us. We all wish to teach our children the importance of telling the truth. We do so because of the desire within each of us to connect with what we know to be right. In this particular case it's dealing with reality. It's facing the truth.

Our source of power knew the effects of reality because He represented it. He knew the consequences of those who chose to resist it or deny it because in doing so they would deny Him. Reality is everywhere at the same time. It never changes because it represents the truth. It doesn't get older or decrease in its effects but continues to uphold the very way in which we were designed to function. To not see it as a measuring tool is to think that life is a one-way street with no options. Our way would be considered the only way, leaving nothing for it to be compared to, which causes us to avoid reality instead of facing it. We have seen in the previous chapter that this is where deception gains its strength. It fights us when we would seek the truth, and it reminds us of our inferiority when we would demand to have the truth revealed to us.

Our power source has provided us with the necessary tools to follow a path designed specifically for us. We as human beings do get off track sometimes and of course we become confused and lose touch with reality but we must not lose sight of what we need to see—the truth. This isn't to be a conflicting attempt to explain the human dilemma of mankind and his inability to make all the right decisions at the right time, but it is meant to acknowledge the true fact that reality comes from the truth and acts as a force in our lives to help keep us from those things that oppose the truth.

Once again, we arrive at the point of the question: Who is this force, which seems to operate everywhere at the same time, which no one can really explain, yet He continues to work; no one can understand, yet He continues to move in ways unknown to what He created. Who is this truth-revealer who shows us the truth when we do not want to see it? Who is this power source who adapts Himself to situations just to prove His point? Who is this source who manifests Himself in all forms, be it music, counseling, doctors, television, or in the common everyday scene of a dream, just to show us glimpses of the hope we should have and the dignity of life we possess as a part of His eternal power?

I still do not wish to debate theologically the issue of whether there is a God and does He exist because it is only obvious that we didn't create ourselves. If we had created ourselves we would be before the beginning. Reality proves to us that we are finite beings. If we were not then we would not need to have things revealed to us because we would already know them. We would not need to ask questions because we would already know the answers. We would be our own representatives because we would know all that we seek and reality would not need to exist because it could not show any new thing.

If reality represents our source of power then we need it to function because to see it is to see our maker. Confusion or insecurity become crystal clear when faced with the truth, and our minds are peaceful and our souls can rest. Aren't these the characteristics which make this force God? One thing is for sure, no matter how much we learn as finite beings or no matter how innovative we become as a nation, we will constantly have to face reality, the truth, and our power source—Our God.

Chapter Four

God and Democracy

Our source of power has prescribed for us the perfect medicine that allows us to recognize the good as well as the bad. He knew that the destiny of mankind depended on the choices they would make. He could not have created such a free-flowing spirit with a string attached to its back, enabling Him to control every action and dictate every thought. We had to be free to make bad decisions, just as we are free to make good decisions. He knew that in doing so priorities would have to be established.

When He created human life, He knew that in order for the level of existence to be maintained, a certain craving would have to exist within the soul of mankind. Creation would have to want its creator just as much as the spirit of the creator wanted to dwell in creation. In order to represent the image of the creator, creation would have to be willing to sacrifice. We all think we know what's best for each of us, only to find that our well-thought-out visions for our lives need the interacting of a greater source in order to come to pass. He had to be the indisputable force with the answers for the dilemma of humankind, just as a building contractor knows the make-up of a building and its materials. He had to know us inside and out in order to demand our trust and faith.

This great power would establish Himself as the ultimate power source of perfection and the intercessor for the maturity of the soul. The soul only develops if it is connected with its original source from the beginning. The true perspective remains a fantasy, without a belief system to serve as a guide throughout life. The very foundation of our beliefs is strengthened by the revelation of the truth.

That belief determines how we define the word *good*. For example, the success of someone may be considered by most to be something good, whereas for the jealous and negatively influenced people, the downfall of those striving for success is considered as something good. This is the difference between the forces that try to influence our minds for the benefit of our source and the other force seeking its own personal glory. The one clings to our God and His characteristics. The other opposes the qualities of our God that it might justify its actions.

One is a carnal spirit that craves the desires of the human flesh. This force seeks to deviate as much as possible from what resembles the good that it might act out its frustrations through our natural desires. All desires are good if used in the way they were meant to be satisfied. But if used based on an endless desire that needs to be fulfilled, darkness and separation are the end results.

Where does all this fit with the title of this chapter, "God versus Democracy"? It defines a compromise between a nation of people who will themselves away from what they proclaim as their defining characteristic. We demand to be understood as One Nation under God Indivisible with Liberty and Justice for All. It is strange to define the foundations of a country upon the truths and beliefs in a higher power without adhering to the very principles of such a power.

Society is strange because it wants to have its cake and eat it too. It likes to walk down the middle of the street without taking one side or the other. It likes to be glorified at the expense of the people. It convicts us of our shortcomings by limiting our opportunities while it makes laws with options, meaning they are only enforced when convenient. It hides behind the dogma that laws are made from humans with limited capacities, and that's why imperfections and injustices go unchallenged and unchanged. That is walking down the middle of the street, avoiding the traffic instead of pointing it in the direction it should go.

Think about it. *One Nation under God.* If we are united, subjected to the greatest being, shouldn't our democracy uphold the spiritual truths that define our freedom and not annul our divine relationship with our creator by allowing the manipulation of free will? Shouldn't a democracy lead its citizens to the truth and not away from it? A democracy, although it is the essence of free will, should not take a back seat to the forces that seek to destroy our communities, neighborhoods, mentalities, and most importantly our souls. Don't be confused with what society allows us to understand. Just because we have the freedom and the right to make our own decisions, we also have an obligation to remain embedded in the truth.

The Source and Foundation of Society

Our personal characteristics define who we are and what we are connected to. If we continue to dismiss the effects of God, using our definition of a democracy as an excuse then our end result is deserved and our ultimate end a disaster. So now we see that God affects the laws of the land relative to the principles upon which it is established. If governmental laws are dictated based on the preferences of its parts and not the integrity of its foundation, then the flaws of the pieces are the end results of manipulation and prejudices, which contradict "and justice for all." I am not saying that a state or a country is responsible for the personal beliefs and acts of its constituents, but I am saying that the governing body should be demonstrators of the subjective power themselves, that sound decisions may be made and the peace of the land may be established.

Before a law can affect a country it must first affect the hearts of its pieces. People form the pieces which make up the whole and if the pieces do not acknowledge the effects of their God, then how can a nation serve as a witness for the truth? The laws upon which countries are founded must represent the source of its supreme being in order to lead people in the direction of their destinies and not down a dark road based on self-fulfillment and self-righteousness. Society doesn't define the existence of God nor the extent of the effect He should have on the people of the land, but God should be the source and foundation upon which society builds its hopes. A democracy is not a new definition of free will or freedom of choice because upon the creation of mankind, this great power gave us what we claim to have established. It was already a characteristic of the great image in which we were created.

Freedom of Choice

To misunderstand the freedom that our source of power has given us is to misrepresent the image in which we were created. It allows us to justify our shortcomings by never taking responsibility for our own actions. We want what we want without experiencing the art of sacrificing and suffering patiently. We want the good without experiencing the bad. We think the bad is a result of an action. We never view the bad as an opportunity to prove the good. Instead we ignore the bad and wish to explain the good. We make laws based on human preferences and not divine rule. We allow discoveries and philosophies to do our thinking for us. The influence of God is seen as an option and not a necessity.

Of course free will is ours to take, but the breath of life was our creator's to give. Therefore, we owe our being to one power and the laws that govern our lands to one source. In light of all of this, we see that subjection is a must for those of us who wish to operate in the power each of us has been given. To be divinely governed, however, doesn't mean we limit our will to succeed or our wishes for the better things in life. This is not the purpose of the boundaries we were given to live within. They were not meant to stop us from achieving the level of completeness we seek, but as our protection against all the opposing forces that attempt to cause us to step outside the boundaries of the truth.

A house without a fence around it is viewed as different from the house with a fence surrounding it. The house without a fence has no protection and anyone can walk directly to the entrance. Laws of society made without the divine consideration are allowing the forces of evil to manipulate the vessels they should protect. The inhabitants of the land become houses without fences, subjected to the forces that rule their empowered decision-makers. Exceptions are made and compromises agreed upon which limit the power of our almighty force to demonstrate His divine qualities in our lives. There is no room for exceptions within the realm of the almighty. We have to accept the ways of what we wish to follow in order to develop trust in what we claim to believe in. We as a country have to pay close attention to the type of laws we make and how we implement them. Freedom of choice is great for a country wishing to build its value system upon God's standards, but to proclaim democracy as an excuse to be indecisive provides lifestyles of "anything goes," rather than the disciplined subjection our supreme force requires.

The Fence of Protection

The definition of a democracy should not be used as an excuse to undermine the creator of mankind. I say *undermine* because to leave room for manipulation of a common law is to remain indecisive. Our house without a fence example paints the picture of having the building in which to live but not having the protection to ensure its endurance. The source of all power is the protection of all that wish to embrace it. It should be the foundation upon which all truth and all laws should be compared. It must rule if the good characteristics of our source are to be accepted or even acknowledged. The fence serves as protection but also as a warning. No one can get to the house except they first go through the fence. Our source of power clearly allows us to understand this for ourselves as He gives us free will to make decisions we know could affect our lives. Our belief in this source allows a fence to protect us. It does not mean that negativity would never try to penetrate or invade our mode of living but it does mean we would be able to recognize the forces for what they are. The fence serves as a boundary. To trust in the creator of such a boundary is what we call faith. Faith in this creator gives us restrictions. But these restrictions are not meant to be seen as limitations but are meant to make us aware of our surroundings.

The Creator's Guidelines

The creator of the land first gives the laws of the land. The developer of any type of product has certain guidelines to follow in order to arrive at the finished product, which meets the intended objective. Of course substitutes can be used in the place of the necessary parts but the authenticity of the product and its capabilities are taken away. Simply put, compromising divine laws with the touch of human likeness serves as a substitute for the original intention of the divine creator. It takes away from the authenticity of the truth and replaces it with a manipulated fact. This divine source has given us what we need to maintain His provisions. Although we are free creatures allowed to make free choices, we cannot and should not remove ourselves from such a covering by denying the power, which seeks only to protect us.

Our world is a mixture of different attitudes that affect the way in which we live. But these different views are necessary that we might all understand the way in which this supreme being works. He has different modes of reception as well as distribution. But His intention is the same for everyone. I do not mean He will make everyone millionaires, because it is not necessary to be a millionaire to live a good life. We need not have lots of anything to feel happy and complete.

Society presents us with vague ideas of what success is and what it means. Our power source also provides us with His view of what success is but we cannot walk down the middle of the street to find it. We have to choose which side of the traffic we wish to blend in with. Be careful, because to choose one side means we will have to sacrifice something, usually our own satisfactions, to meet His, which in turn we will find more pleasing to our soul.

To choose the other side is to walk unprotected. We forfeit our protection and power to recognize the truth, when it attempts to reveal itself. And worse than that, we become blind to the forces which seek to destroy our soul. As a result of these factors, we fail to realize the truth as it pertains to a democracy. We fail to understand that a democracy indeed is the freedom of choice but it is also founded upon the first fruits of what is considered to be right. If this is the case and we understand right to come from our source of power, then man-made laws should not manipulate the original law, causing us to walk down the middle of the street, but it should uphold the original intentions of the good without options.

Explaining the Unknown

I do not wish to critically state the imperfections of human beings, I just want to make clear why humanistic views without intricate assistance from our source provide opportunities to fail before giving us a reason to succeed. Power has to be recognized for what it is, a characteristic given to us from our source of power. It serves the purpose for which it was intended that we might accept it and not manipulate or abuse it.

Governmental authorities serve as a defining quality of our creator because they are to align themselves up with their source in order to carry out the instructions designed for them. This good power is the source of all good things. Along with the right kind of power comes many things: peace of mind, which we all need to think and operate clearly; security, which of course assures us of the support of our maker at all times so that we never feel alone; self-confidence, which never allows us to give up on anything even when the light looks dim at the end of the tunnel.

This power source never tries to make us think we will live trouble-free lives but rather that trouble sets the stage for His power to be revealed. He can of course remove the trouble out of the way but then we would never get a chance to watch Him prove Himself. We would never have a reason to believe in His power because we would never see the end result of His work. Instead as forces tend to oppose the truth, whether through human laws or political reigns of what we term a democracy, they still cannot deny Him although they seek to operate on their own.

So we see once again that be it a higher power or whatever name some of us want to give it, it exists and will not cease to exist. And no matter where we turn, we see His awesome power. Have you ever looked at the details in which the earth is formed? Scientists, theorists, and theologians become inspired seekers of the good, wishing to explain such perfection. We cannot get enough of trying to explain the unknown.

But is He unknown? If He made creation in His image shouldn't we at least be able to see Him through mankind? Acts of good manners, from opening up the car door for the less fortunate to respectfully responding when someone greets us, are a sign of the good that dwells in each of us. To not be able to explain something does not mean that it doesn't exist. It just means it's beyond our human capacity to comprehend, which makes it a greater source of power in which we should trust and not question.

Does this power source represent democracy? It does if democracy doesn't manipulate the truth. As I said before, we consider ourselves one nation under God, indivisible with liberty and justice for all. To be under God we have to accept the guidelines He sets. We should not try to detract from His laws to arrive at what we consider good. It must be His laws, without options.

I am not trying to lash out at the government of our country, I just need to say that if we consider God our God then we ought to let Him be God, and we ought to institute the very beliefs which we proclaim as the foundation of this country, not just for ourselves but also for the surrounding countries who look to us for support. This is what constitutes a great nation, not a booming economy or a bunch of successful people who hide behind their secret beliefs. If we want Him, He is there to direct and to redirect. Even when we choose to forget Him He is still right beside us hoping one day, as a people and as a nation, we will give Him a chance to make a difference in our lives.

Is this higher power God? If He is not He sure fools me every time I wake up and see the bright blue skies or the rain that waters His earth. He sure tricks me when my heart yearns to hear His voice that I might find peace. Is He who He says He is? If not He is the best actor in the history of the world. So is He God? I think so. One thing is for sure, He is greater than we are and commands our respect and submission.

Chapter Five

Fear, Doubt, and Unbelief

The greatest reason not to believe in the truth is be afraid of the risk involved in believing in it. If our minds can be influenced by forces which oppose our good source, then we must seek to understand why such a force wishes to interrupt our relationship with our greater source. What does this force not want us to see? What is it trying to keep us from finding out? As stated before this is not an equal and opposing force to our beginning power. If so this force would also at times have complete control of creation and would not need to use negative forces as avenues for its power.

In order to believe in anything, we begin by searching for other ways in which to express our inner secrets, only to find that one way supersedes them all. We experiment and explore other avenues before arriving at the truth. We sometimes walk in a circle when we should be walking a straight line. Along the way we have an encounter with a power source that not only rejuvenates our energy but also clarifies our journey into the unknown. Before we become what we were destined to be, we all have been lost and in need of direction. We all have been afflicted and tempted in one way or another.

The forces of the good source which desires our soul are challenged by the negative forces which feed our desires and only gain momentum when we yield to temptation. There is one thing we have to remember. The good forces rule and are the reflection of the first divine intention of mankind. Negative forces could not have been created first because then we would be considered greater than the good source. This would say that our human nature is the intended nature when really it is not, if our purpose in our existence is to love.

Love is not a characteristic of a negative force; hate is. Believe it or not, most of our first reactions are not those of hate. We usually respond in a hateful way because of what we allow to affect us. But the original intention is good. This means our original nature is that which conforms to our beginning source. Usually we hate something because it threatens us in some manner. We can't understand it so we choose to dislike it. Instead of confronting the issue which generates this fear, we leave it to grow and grow and grow, making us communicatively incompetent.

Fear Contradicts Our Supreme Power

Now fear, as a characteristic of this negative force, tries to function in our life as an obstacle. Fear is the opposite of love, power, and soundness of mind. It haunts our self-confidence; it attacks our self-esteem. Nothing is ever right; we never see the good in anything; in all of our seeking to explain the most simple facts fear finds a way to distort the truth, that things may not be revealed as they were intended to be.

To find the common good is to recognize the opposing bad and resist it. Not to do so is like watching a snowball begin its descent and never stopping it until it's too late. Influenced by fear, we look over our shoulder when there is nothing to see. We think monsters exist when it is just a facet of our imagination. Fear is a characteristic of a negative force used to distort our emotions, so that what we think is true cannot be accepted, and the good that we would do, we find not to be worth the trouble.

Therefore, we present our own obstacles by allowing fear to rule when it should submit to our greater force. This negative power source seeks to consume our good energy that it may be used for bad energy. This source had to have known our supreme power because it contradicts every mission He tries to implement. It would not do so if it did not know the true goodness this power has to offer. This negative force tries constantly to intercept the intended good lest we accept it and grow away from the negative force. It seeks to use us against what we learned to be our new way.

This fear is proposed that we might all make choices. It challenges the strength we proclaim to have. We state claims of our makeup as human beings, relating to good and bad qualities, only to have our every word challenged and tried by the opposing force. This force must use fear as a way to stop us from following what we believe in because in, doing so we reject the very power we were given and function as a one-dimensional being instead of the two-fold creatures we are. We see things one way and we forget the very image in which we were created. We all have to make up our own minds because this is the essence of what life is all about. We also have to agree that this force could not like us to want to use us against the truth. It could not have our best interest at heart if it only seeks to fulfill its own satisfactions through us.

Doubt Uses Fear to Cause Unbelief

Doubt is also a negative characteristic of this negative power. Doubt doesn't allow us to trust or even carefully consider the choices we have before us. It causes us to wonder and to always remain skeptical of what's presented to us. Therefore, we never believe the truth even when it's staring us right in the face. Doubt and unbelief are tied together because they affect each other. Doubt uses fear to cause unbelief.

These three characteristics could not possibly have come from our initial power because that would mean He never intended for us to be like Him. He would have war with Himself if each part of His character contradicted the other. He could not make anything in His image because He would be confused as to which image He wanted to represent. And we could not be held accountable for any of our actions if our source never defined the truth of life.

Can we term this force an enemy? Before we answer this question, let's consider an example. A competitor is one who competes for a common outcome. A winner is the one who overcomes the attributes of the others to stand alone. An enemy tries to blend in with the common good to infiltrate it for the use of his own wishes. An enemy wants to take what we have directly and indirectly. He doesn't want to compete; he wants to cheat. He wants to be called a winner but he does not want to live like a winner. So to answer the question, let's define the actions of the enemy.

An enemy tries to distract, manipulate, connive, and intrude in a form of what appeals to us. He studies us but our true creator already knows us. This negative force has to find our weaknesses whereas this all-knowing creator knew what our weaknesses would be when He made us. This force which opposes the truth must indeed be the enemy of our good source. It needs our human body to live and to act out its frustrations relative to the divine order, the original purpose we all have been created to fulfill. The positive force wants to use our human body for His good and ours, but ultimately He can exist on His own. There is a difference. The one has to have you in order to inflict confusion to your state of mind but the other would love to have you trust and believe so that you recognize the use of fear, doubt, and unbelief as obstacles, which we all have the power to overcome.

Now we can have a better understanding of this great image in which we were created. He has power to overcome all forces which oppose His existence. Therefore, He gave mankind, which is made after His image, the power to also overcome by recognizing the opposing forces which seek to manipulate the intended good of mankind.

Confrontation Is Not Optional

Once again we arrive at the point of self-control, the ability to make choices for one's own good in the midst of distractions and confrontations. Fear, doubt, and unbelief are all challenges to self-control. We all have the power to operate correctly without becoming discouraged or dismayed at whatever our situations may be. Fear, doubt, and unbelief are now exposed and they only have as much power as we give them.

Confrontation is not an option—it is a necessity if we are to function in the power in which we were given. Our creator would not create us to fail, although He may allow us to be tempted. He allows it so that our proclamations will have value and substance, which gives us strength. Confrontation helps us learn and seek the face of this true power, causing us to be curious as to His existence and our beginning. This is the exact point we all must get to in order to believe in what we find. Our faith becomes not just a religious quality but a commonality as it relates to true life.

So we see that as many differences as society points out in each of our lives, there is one thing that we all have in common: we all have an enemy. We all have an opposing force, which doesn't care about our families or our income brackets. This force is not concerned about the many material things we believe are necessary to have in order to feel important. Instead, this force tries to misconstrue what are supposed to be positive attributes in our lives and tries to put us at difference with ourselves and each other so that we do not consider the good but manipulate it for our own satisfactions.

This negative force loves to dwell in groups because there is the greatest power of influence. To stand alone and state a fact doesn't convince everyone that what we speak is the truth. But if more than one person expresses the same opinions, then that proclamation now has quality. Friends can be great but they can also be obstacles. Every one of us would like to have that confidant, that person we can trust with our feelings or secrets. But friends can become obstacles when they don't share our views about certain things, creating a gap and leaving room for misunderstandings about the simplest things. And now the person we shared our most intricate emotions with not only has our heart in their hands but also a weapon to use against us.

This negative force thrives on this type of manipulation. It does so by trying to convince us to be a part of the group by participating in the group activity, although we feel completely out of place and uncomfortable. The most lasting scars to our souls are questioned and left to remain in the category of the unknown just by wondering what people will think of us if we don't follow the crowd. This is why we need not fear the lonely walk if it means peace to our souls. We shouldn't doubt the positives that come from remaining embedded in a solid foundation just because the quick road to success seems to be traveled by many. We are to wait patiently for the right time, when our source of power will provide for us the true necessities of life and not the temporary things that have no substance.

Higher Connection Before Personal Pleasure

We have all had great imaginations of what we thought would be the ultimate experience in life only to find that the reality of such fantasies was a complete nightmare. We thought drinking with our buddies was a cool thing to do until the morning after. We thought one puff on a cigarette elevated our respect amongst our peers, only to need a stronger substance to sustain our common departures from reality. Such a negative force tries to change our good thoughts into bad experiences so that we might not believe that any good thing comes to those who follow the truth.

It is amazing how many drug addicts would be free from their source of dependency if they recognized the negative forces which convinced them that they had reason and an excuse for what they are doing. The thoughts are mind-boggling to imagine the teenage pregnancies that occur out of curiosity and the inability to control desires manipulated by negative forces. If this force of persuasion was exposed and not allowed to convince us of personal pleasure before higher connection, then self-control would gain momentum and a greater foundation would be established.

What about the wedge that is driven between husbands and wives? This force seeks to divide and persuade so that the original intention for creation would lie in the hands of a "have it your way" type of society. How about the philosophies of obedience? This force confuses the minds of the parents so that acts of disobedience go unpunished for fear of what society will say and what the child will do. This fear leads us away from what we should control. It ultimately becomes a reflection upon our households as each maturing adult takes the same untamed attitudes into a society that acts as a dictatorship, instead of subjecting itself to the very principles it claims to be the backbone of all of its statutes and creeds.

Don't be deceived. This force operates and lives in every negative statistic that is revealed. Most statistical categories reveal how bad a thing is, rather than how good it is. It's kind of like letting the negative forces know how well they are doing. For example, 50 percent of all marriages end in divorce. I am not saying we shouldn't report issues. I'm only expressing the mode of attack as it relates to negative forces.

We who seek and find our source of power find peace for our soul and a foundation that recognizes and exposes every negative force trying to reveal itself through us. In a nutshell, we break generational curses and instill the peace of our creator into the hearts of creation when we allow Him to dwell in us that we might reflect the power of an invisible force by our visible actions.

We, as a nation, are to find individual peace that we may distribute worldwide peace. The pieces of the puzzle make up the puzzle but if the pieces lack the fitting quality to complete the whole, the end result is confusion and not harmony. Peace agreements are fine, but let's make sure the peace we seek meets our standards, because only then can we understand how to have peace or even how to recognize it when it appears.

Chapter Six

Idolatry

To trust in something so much that it becomes the standard by which our belief system functions will cause us to live a life based only on what we create, and not in the established truth. The established truth is the foundation for all things. It is the energy giver for all sources of power. Without it we live unguided, disguised, and unprotected lives. If we trust in what we humanly can create, we become blind leaders of the blind because our minds are limited and incapable of being totally satisfied. It's one thing to allow a priority to have significant value in our lives but it is another to make something of no value a significant priority in our lives.

The Essence of Life

Before our minds run away with us, let me explain a bit. We all have sports heroes as well as established habits and values. The only time our attitudes towards our sports heroes change is when they reveal a part of their human side that makes us understand that, although gifted, they are fighting the same mind-boggling temptations that we are. We set them on a pedestal because they reveal a higher connection. They seem to contain what we seek. Therefore, we strive to have what they have so that we might feel the peace of accomplishment. In doing so we lose ourselves in other human beings. Their interest becomes ours. Their strategies become ours. Our priorities only matter when they are ours because they affect us first and the outside world second. We have to be careful not to give significant value to something that shouldn't be a priority in our lives. We cannot live through others but we can learn from others that we might transfer the positives from their lives into ours, and that we might use the negative experiences they share as stepping stones for a better way.

Our habits and values fall along the same principles. Some of us go to church out of habit. We have been doing it for so long that we forgot that we were supposed to get something out of it. Some of us do the same thing every weekend because that's just the way it's been for years. Some of us never express our concerns because we are used to going along with the crowd. We become more crowd pleasers than right-way seekers.

Things that shouldn't take us by force become the most important things in our lives. Competition drives us to the point of death and debt. Jealousy creates negative views and selfishness. To love becomes a cold-hearted feeling instead of the warm inner peace it should bring. To make the meaningless meaningful creates a problem for mankind. To trust more in a perishable thing than the creator of all things places a division between the potter and the clay. We should never try to substitute the necessary with the unnecessary. We do ourselves an injustice by doing so.

An idol is whatever is most important to us. It is what we spend most of our time thinking about. It is what we spend most of our time dreaming about. An idol is what we give top value to. We place it above all that matters. For some of us, idols are our habits. We spend more time with them, doing them, or thinking about them than anything else. We make idols out of material things. Things that pass away day after day, we hold genuine in our hearts as if they represent our lives. Our addictions become our idols because we feel overruled and overpowered by such controlled substances that consume our time and our lives.

Our families, as important as they are, sometimes rule more of our lives than they should. We think that as long as our families agree with what we have and what we do, then that makes everything alright. An idol is dangerous because it becomes the ruler of our thoughts. We have made it so because it occupies the most important part of existence—time. After all, an idol only has value and power if we allow it to.

Let's not be mistaken here, an idol is not necessarily a gold figure made to resemble the stature of a being. It can be a lustful appetite, riotous living, a bad attitude, or the will to do whatever it takes to succeed. The beauty of making a god of like substances is the ability to pick it up and put it down whenever we want. We can see it, so we can use it however and whenever we want. This takes away the need to have faith and patience because all that we want we also control. In this case, faith in a greater source is not necessary because what we see is now our strength or our meaning in life.

Our conscience bears us witness because it is never convicted or challenged. Anything superficial caters to wants and selfish desires and not the state of contentment and satisfaction we all claim to seek. Idols have no power but give a false sense of hope as they are allowed to substitute for what we are not willing to wait for. The idol's actions or power isn't dependent upon its capabilities. It's all dependent upon what we make it out to be, which in reality is a created facet of our imagination. It fills a void that we want filled. Instead of searching the depths of our soul to find our beginning source, we have created our own source.

Anything created by mankind is limited and therefore is called an idol if it receives more of our time than our true source does. Anything created cannot give us the peace we seek because it doesn't know how. It doesn't know us. We are tricking ourselves if we claim an intervention from a higher source while creating our own source of power. We are merely fooling ourselves if we proclaim the mountains of blessings, but behind the rocks are hidden wishing wells.

Peace of mind is the greatest comfort to the soul because it allows us to see things through the eyes of the truth. This does not mean hardships and the difficulties of life never try our strength as human beings but we see each trial for what it is and we are able to operate with the serenity which our greater source has given us.

To worship something is to want to be like it. It is to be willing to sacrifice our thoughts and ambitions in order to match that which we wish to emulate. Our sight is fastened on it and the very sense of life and significance we give it seems to provide for us a false sense of power. So the amount of power this idol has is directly related to us. Like anything, however much time we give to something usually determines the amount of power the thing has. It's a cop-out, so to speak, trying to please the aspirations of human consumption instead of the divine power of our beginning source.

Filling the Void

We as humans tend to create whatever we feel to be a void in our lives. For example, when we need encouragement we tend to seek those who will provide such a need. When we need direction we find those who wish to lead us in the way we should to go. When we need to feel empowered by our own talents, we choose to listen to those who will stroke our egos.

The same principles apply when we seek to try to understand the existence of a higher power. We have to get into position to hear what our source has to say about our needs before we take matters into our own hands. But this type of access can only be unlocked with the key of faith. A faithful key will cause us to wait for the revelation of the truth. A faithful key will jump-start our engines just enough to keep us going so that we do not neglect the eternal forces of life, that we might live and not die, not physically, but detached from reality and entrapped in a web of deceit.

A Distortion of the Created Good

An idol is nothing but a created comfort, acting as a substitute for what truly exists. This is the dilemma of mankind as it relates to belief and trust in what cannot be seen, but yet is more dependable than what mankind creates. Our human minds are at constant work to understand the inerrant power of our creator. As a result we become frustrated and impatient and do greatly err in making the power of an incorruptible image into that of what He created.

For a more modern way of understanding what an idol is, look at what we put most of our trust in. Money indeed is necessary to live and to help others in need but once it becomes so important that one is willing to sacrifice all just to have it, that goes beyond what is necessary. The medium of exchange has become an idol. It has taken on a mind of its own and at all cost we will do anything to have it, even if it means resenting the power source which provided the medium to fulfill our need.

Houses are wonderful, especially if we can build or find one to fit our personal preferences. However, once it becomes a goal to impress instead of a place of comfort, our cherished hopeful becomes a kink in the path of satisfaction. Job titles are needful because they explain and outline each task and the expected levels of performance. A job is a position of service, not one of kingship, and it should be remembered that respect of persons should be common to all, not relative to the position he or she holds. I picked these three, money, homes, and job titles because they seem to be the common goals of every person alive today. These are not bad desires or goals, don't misunderstand me here, but I wish to point out the fact that our trust should not rest in these perishable things more than our faith in our only true power source.

These goals become idols when we focus on them instead of using them as a reflection of what our power source has created for us. Yes, I say in which our power source has created for us because we have already agreed that for the common good to exist it had to come from the source of good. Since an evil force tries to intervene between creation and creator then that which is good spells out success. If success is seen as good then it can only come from that which is good. And if this source of power is all-powerful, then truly He has the knowledge and the power to bring to pass all that He has foreseen.

Even when bad things happen, this all-mighty power still has the power to bring the good out of the bad. Success is termed the end result of hard work because the good source uses the bad challenges to build character and substance. Once the level of success is reached, the barricades of idolatry cannot influence the situation because the trial of belief by the truth brought out the best in us. The best in us is not us but it is the image in which we were created.

It has to be because our fallen nature as human beings prevents us from knowing all that we should and brings us to a point of decision making. Whether we will develop our own way or not, which in many instances causes us to determine what matters and what doesn't, we are relying upon our own principles to establish the essence of the truth. This is the result of our own decision making. We rely upon our own mind to satisfy a need.

Is this power source greater than an idol? I think so since an idol is man-made whereas this all knowing source of power is not. The need to have a verifiable figure in the form of what our imagination imagines gives us a false sense of security. This power source is and forever will be questioned because no one can figure Him out. An idol is different because the imaginable thoughts, which make up its existence, also define its limitations. It can do no more than we believe it to be able to and, as we discussed earlier, deception now works with our imagination, confusing and abusing the intended good, causing us to miss the truth even though it's staring us right in the face.

Money which was provided as a medium of exchange now becomes the abuse of a need, allowing greed to enter, distorting contentment, and sacrificing its intended good. A house becomes a status symbol instead of a comfortable place of peace and therefore the bigger and the better leads to emptiness and insecurity. The job title begins to serve as a position of power, separating the classes of humanity and forming the different prejudices that form our culture today. Idolatry becomes a distortion of the intended good.

Back to Our Original State

There is nothing wrong with being highly successful to the point of the acquisition of many material goods. The only problem is when the material goods begin to define the personhood of the individual. In these cases, the foundation of a person is weak and influenced to the point of not being able to use what was meant to be a sign of achievement. Our limited minds begin to associate a particular lifestyle with what we imagine, leaving out the essence that proves its truth, that of acknowledging the creator of such good.

So could this all-knowing power be replaceable? That would be impossible unless it was replaced with a force of equal power. Anything less would not be acceptable nor accessible since its makeup is of a limited substance. An idol as a god, material possessions as worshipping symbols, or even positions of authority as status acceptance would only say that these things are limited sources which hinder advancement.

If this good source of power meant for what He created to live in a perfect way, by protecting and instructing them and even saving them from destruction, then what would be the point of reconciling something which was lost if the intention was not to bring it back to its original state? That would mean that since the beginning of time, death had no reign, but after the fall of humanity our eternal state was temporarily interrupted. That doesn't change the fact that our initial state should be the goal of every soul. Now we would have a new beginning which was an old beginning reestablished, giving us the eternal opportunity we were meant to have from the beginning of time. Arguably possible, within the minds of our limited intelligence probably, but in the minds of those who can relate to such a power source, this is and was the intention of such an awesome power.

Idolatry

Is this source God? He is everything an idol is not—the truth. But is he God? He is the very strength upon which the earth rotates. Yes, I hear you, but is He God? He is not only the reason we are alive or have the ability to breathe, but He is the source of life, of which nothing can exist without Him. Yes, He is God and we see Him everyday.

We feel Him when our heart beats and we acknowledge Him when we smile. We relate to Him when we cry. We exemplify Him when we hold to what we know to be true. We emulate Him when we express love. We acknowledge His intentions when we institute righteousness in the place of evilness. Whether we choose to believe Him or not, He exists and in one way or another we define a part of the good characteristics of a higher source.

An idol is a false implication of what exists. It cannot be a god because it doesn't qualify. It is merely a facet of our imagination. Those who want to be worshipped in a godly way must first act as a god. A god is perfect and his existence is not contingent upon any thing. People who make themselves gods are spiritual wanna-be's because they are neither equipped nor capable of operating as the true power source of something which they didn't create.

Be careful what you follow or what you believe, because just as the magician deceives us, we may follow a tradition or a cliché and in the end discover it never existed. So once again, does this higher force exist? Absolutely. Upon it hangs the beginning and end of a thing and in it lies the substance of what we consider the truth. We have to look in the mirror and open our hearts, be honest with ourselves, and ask, *is there such a power which rules with dominance and grace to the saving of the soul?* We have to be sure our answer is true because this determines our outlook and our faith and more importantly our belief in whether this higher power is who He says He is—God.

Chapter Seven

Love vs. Hate

*L*ove. Just to think of it brings soothing to our souls. It is like sunshine on a cloudy day. It heals the inflicted wounds. It gives us constant hope in the midst of a bird's-eye view of opportunity. It brings calmness to the mind of the frustrated. It brings clearness to the path of injustice. It fills our hearts with joy and at the same time with tears. Love is strong and cannot be overlooked. It cries for recognition. It wishes to be expressed and to sit at the forefront, for with it are the issues of life. It must rule as the only action of expression in order to represent the source of its character. It cannot change. If it could it would be a conditional trait making it impossible to be whole. It doesn't criticize except for the acknowledgment of the truth. It draws humans together, forming bonds, which endure the toughest afflictions. It unites the clay with its potter. It separates the truth from a lie. It is often described as the greatest feeling in the world, and rightfully so, because it comes from the greatest being the world has ever known.

A Big Smile with Evil Intentions

Love cannot hate because hate is not a part of its quality or characteristic. Hate in fact contradicts love and seeks to overrule the emotional state of the intended good so that feelings determine actions. This is what we term hypocritical. Our feelings should never determine our actions because feelings change too often.

Hate seeks to infiltrate the minds of those who would be so used for the good. It wants us to find differences and hold on to the prejudices, which divide and not unite. Hate has a big smile with evil intentions. It wants us to believe one thing so that it can show us another. The force of hate will not allow us to move past our problems but will find a way for us to feel secure in our situations by placing the blame for our shortcomings on someone else. These characteristics are used by the evil forces to prove that the good, which exists in each of us, is always challenged with the bad, which desires to operate through us.

We are at constant crossroads regarding the decisions we are to make and the roads we have to take. True enough, our destiny is affected by what we believe. But to believe something without proclaiming it is like having all the answers to an exam but never writing them down. It is not enough just to believe in something. We have to be ready to be challenged by the opposing forces by standing up for what we believe in, even if it might cost us our lives. Many of you reading this book probably feel I'm a little detached from reality after this last comment. However, our strength lies in what we are willing to do because of our beliefs, not how many people reassure us relative to our beliefs. Speaking allows us to take one side and not remain indecisive.

The problem with this is once we decide to speak what we know to be true, we are challenged by what we profess. For the one force, the necessary faith needed to follow His lead is strengthened by the challenges of opposing forces if the proclaimer holds to the words spoken. If we never profess the truth in our hearts then our hearts will never be tried. Our words will just be words and we will have no substance upon which our words will hang.

Hate won't allow us to see the good. It tries to challenge our minds constantly, so that curiosity does not become our doorway to salvation. Just being curious causes us to seek for what we feel is missing. Love provides reasons for us to continue the search whereas hate projects obstacles, as minor preventions to turn us away from what many of us are not far from. Love gives us a mind-set to want to know the power of our creator and He does it by allowing us to ponder the limitations of mankind, causing us to believe that a greater source is in control.

Then He shows us the natural good of the earth in its purest form causing our curiosities to be challenged by what we now see. As we get closer to this awesome power, we begin to understand that the qualities of love which we considered the definition of the highest feeling are the very essence of His character. We find then that love dwells with this higher power and rules with Him. It is what caused our curiosity. It is what challenged the opposing forces, which would not let go of us. Everything we thought about love exists with this source. He showed it to us just by creating His own opportunity to come to us.

What makes us so special? There has to be something or else this evil force, which uses all contradicting powers, would not be so interested in fighting with us or trying to distract us. Hate sees an opportunity to act out its frustrations because our nature is appealing to it. After all, it was man's own knowledge which led him to become detached from perfection in the first place, setting the stage for the intrusion of hateful qualities.

Love Patiently Waits for Us

This is a human problem not a racial one or even a cultural one. All forms of mankind are susceptible to the same things, and the forces of love and hate desire to have each one of them. The situation is simple. Love wants us and can have us but it depends on us and our willingness to want Him. It depends on the affection and the realization we have invested in the curiosity of our soul as to how much seeking we will do for the truth. Love wants us and will do everything to make us aware that He exists. But He will not force or manipulate our mind-set just to be able to possess our heart and soul.

Hate can't really have us so it has to manipulate and trick us into believing in the forces that oppose the truth. It can only persuade us by using our past history or even our current shortcomings as means to keep us from facing the truth. Hate knows we have the power because of the image we reflect. Hate hates us just because we look like that great power. When we smile he wants to present something that will change our smiles to frowns. When we constantly believe the truth will be revealed in due time, he wants to present us with people who do not serve as helpmeets to aid in the solution of the problem but people who become the problem.

We set goals for ourselves as an intelligent person should but somehow doubt sets in and tries to discourage us.

Fear of failing begins to gain momentum and slowly we begin to question our own capabilities. Hate has no interest in our welfare and wants us to not be concerned with anyone but ourselves. To love is to distribute love constantly with the hope that it might become contagious, that all may be infected with the intended good. Hate places one race ahead of the other. He uses classes to define what success is. He gets thrills out of seeing suicidal victims and those who compromise their own beliefs just to be a part of a group. He uses self-esteem as an avenue to destroy one's confidence. Manipulation is his right-hand man and confusion is his best buddy.

    He wants to blind our eyes to change so that we may remain embedded in age-old traditional views, that he can continue his normal generational scam of seek and destroy. He wants doubt to become our companion and jealousy our lifelong roommate. If these attributes of hate's character become realities in our lives, then hate gains strength, which doesn't stop there. He isn't satisfied with bits and pieces of our lives but seeks to sift all the life out of us by turning us against what we should draw closer to.

    He doesn't like us but he sure acts like it. After all, everything he suggests is satisfying to the eyes and to the desires. Hate requires no commitment, just the willingness to be available for use at any time. He doesn't mind our being church regulars; he just doesn't want church to become top priority in our lives. It isn't going to church that bothers him; it's when our life starts to reflect what church presents. He doesn't mind our marrying a wife or husband just as long as we make ourselves available for his use whenever he wishes.

    He wants us to overreact. He wants us to have pity parties because of the possibilities for greater influence, that he might carve his way into the expression of his desires. Hate tries to take from us what love guarantees to us. Love leads us in the way in which we should go, only hoping that we follow. The decision is ours. Just as the right way through obedience to the truth brings about rewards, so disobedience brings with it a just weight.

Love warns us about hate, but hate tries to prevent us from getting to love. Love is so confident in its power that it is able to overcome all odds and operate in places in which it was thought to be shut out of. Love is patient and waits for us. Hate lies in wait for us, not wanting to face us because we just might expose him. He is really afraid of us because we have power to defeat him. He knows it and that is why he tricks and connives his way into our hearts. Love provides the ability to accept the truth and the possibilities of exercising the very power source we all have access to. He wants to give us everything He has, for our good. Hate wants to use us as distributors so that he can infect others with his diseases, which oppose every good thing.

Love has only one outcome. There are no options with love. There are no tricks to be pulled or games to be played. We cannot manipulate love because it is the characteristic of our all-knowing power. It represents the ultimate feeling of expression and the deliverance of a confessed action. It is the truth. It always stands the test of time.

Love Wants to Be Known

Are these two characteristics equivalent with that of the Supreme Being? One is. The other is not. A straight path runs between the two. On each side of us is a decision to be made.

Hate is not a quality of one's characteristic, but a negative aspect of ones choice. We decide to hate or to allow the forces of its kind to cause us to become deceived or blinded. We decide to love as an act of expression forming a bond of strength. Love lifts us up; hate tears us down. When someone loves it is like the shot heard round the world, but when someone hates it becomes like the quiet whispers in the night. It is so because whispers symbolize secrets and insecurities. Love wants to be known because it is what dreams are made of. Hate wants to hide that the ignorant might allow him to rise up to speak.

To be different from what is known as common is not a problem, but to resist the common good to embrace the bad is the power of a negative force. So we are at the point of the question again, could this power source be all that He claims to be if He allows opposing forces to infiltrate and to destroy what He claims He loves? He is once again all that He claims to be because to rule over us is to present Himself to us individually and then on the scale of life as it is seen through others. To love us is to allow us to choose. If He never gave us the freedom of choice then we would not be a people after His image but robots designed to follow instructions. No true god makes us do anything. He presents us with options giving us the opportunity to make up our own mind. During this process, He also shows us parts of His power through which His being is seen. He does so that we might not have the opportunity to deny His reign.

Therefore, He allows us to love so that we may understand His feeling for us and the extent to which His heart yearns to keep us near. We could not love without this characteristic of our almighty power. We could not recognize hate without first knowing love. Whether we choose to acknowledge His existence or not, we do so by the very way we express our highest feelings. As much as cults try to redefine the figure of religious dominance, they can never take away the beginning of all things. The sad part is that religious ignorance brings with it hateful influences, which gather in groups to be heard, and in doing so ruin the way of the weak and destroy the eyes of the hopeful. Without the love of our power source, we would all be mere imitations of what should have been. Is he God? He sure is and He is the epitome of what love is made of.

Chapter Eight

The Past vs. the Present

It is important for us as people to have something in our lives to reflect upon. We need to see for ourselves the different stages of our lives in order to be able to see the process of growth. If this almighty power source only allowed us to have a present state then we would not be able to acknowledge His divine intervention and we would not be able to understand our own achievements. Although not many of us wish to reflect upon our mishaps it is not a bad thing to rediscover our shortcomings in order to avoid making the same mistakes twice.

Think about it—the past is not always a negative. It also serves as a pathway for improvement toward perfection.

The Essence of Life

We as human beings need a past that we might appreciate our current state. We need to be able to look back from time to time to see how far we've come and to be able to recognize the creditor to which we are indebted. To not be free of our past is to live with a dark cloud over our heads, wishing for a better day. We have a choice as it relates to our past; we can recognize the negative forces which tried to misguide us or we can continue in the same field of destruction using fear of not knowing what the future holds as an excuse to remain in our own comfort zones. In fact, we are to learn from what used to control us, that we might not become ignorant to the same devices and also that we might encourage others who seem to be struggling with the same forces of evil. Our past experiences were not just for our own self-enlightenment. They serve as an information center filled with the results of facing the truth.

In order to have a future, we all have to deal with our past. For some of us, this involves fear, childhood disappointments, lack of discipline, and any other distractive experiences which seek to keep us idle instead of moving full steam ahead. Most of us feel that our past gives us reason not to reach for the stars or expect the best out of every situation only to find in the end that what we considered a reason turned out to be an excuse.

How do some people find the way to operate in such power, and others struggle and reject what we all have access to? We all know what taking a risk means. It is acting upon information without being sure of the outcome. Some people find happiness because they risk having their feelings hurt. Some people never find happiness because they never take the risk. How bad do you want what you want in order to risk being disappointed? Relating to this power source, how bad do you want to know Him? Will you risk being foolish by believing that He actually created all that you see, even though others challenge your beliefs with logical explanations of why things are the way they are? You make the call. You have to because your faith is on the line and your call for deliverance is in jeopardy of becoming an empty shadow because you won't speak out.

This is the difference between those who operate in such a high power and those who just believe He exists. Are you a person who makes things happen, a person who watches things happen, or a person who wonders what happened? Your answer to these questions will allow you to determine if your works in this life are results of your faith, or if you refuse to align your life with what you believe.

Our Past Brings Us to Him

How does the past relate to this beginning power source and how does He use it for the good? Our ultimate source of power is the past and the present. He is the past because there isn't anything that happened that He didn't witness, and there isn't anything that was that He didn't know about. That's right, He was there when we took our first drink or our first puff on the cigarette. He even saw us when we had sex for the first time and continued life as if our innocence never left us. Our past is our personal challenge to find our beginning source of power. It haunts us at times because our quest to unite with our source turns our negatives into positives and sets the stage for our change. Only through it can we see our life in retrospect, recognizing when and where some force entered into our lives. This higher power would have to have been present in the past in order to see that we needed an opportunity to change. We would not need to have a force impact our lives if everything was perfect in its initial state.

Our past can also be our obstacle to our future. There are some things which affect us and occupy what seems to be a permanent place in our hearts, keeping us from what we need to survive and hindering us from accepting the truth. This higher being has to be operative here because only He can provide us with the strength to overcome. He also causes us to see our lives in retrospect so that we may use our past as a balancing tool upon which our decisions can be made.

What could this higher power teach us from our past? How about how to survive in the midst of a confused state of mind. Our most immature state of mind is that of our past because we operated then without any restraints and under our own influence. Our past was a sign of a need for something better. If our past state was the ultimate state and without flaws, then there would be no need for change. But since change is a necessary road for us all to take, it alone testifies to our inability to bring ourselves unto the knowledge of the truth.

Our power source uses our past to bring us to Him. Throughout our maturity with each passing day, we find ourselves in situations where not even our parents, friends, or counselors or even our churches can help us. It is then that our cry releases the strength needed to overcome or reveals to us the direction or road we must travel. Our present state is one of triumph. It serves as one of trust and faith. Our present state gives us peace. It gives us hope and it brings us closer to our natural good, that of our original state as it relates to our beginning source of power.

Living in the Past

It is important for us as people to understand the use of the past and the present because it presents itself in the form of the old versus the new. As children we had a certain way of thinking but as we became older the things we used

The Past vs. the Present

to think acquired new meaning and the effect was different. Our past was unstable whereas our present state tends to be more stable. If our lives are to reflect the interactions of emotions and our beliefs, then we all have to encounter something greater in order to believe that there is a better way. This forms our past experience, which aids in our current development. Who could know such a thing except the creator of mankind?

Our minds are limited and that is why we are never sure of what we say or what we do. In this insecure state, this all-knowing power presents us with options. He never chooses for us, but just gives us hints. He gives us hints that we might move from one stage in life to the next—so that we might have a past and a present. We make this transition without having any idea of our destination. Then once we arrive at our desired position, we can take no credit ourselves, but owe it to a higher power.

Sure we think about our own talents and abilities as we journey through the different courses of life but we always find ourselves in dilemmas, needing a helping hand. And for some strange reason during the most difficult times in our lives, we manage only to see one set of footprints. The strangest thing is that we think the set of footprints is ours. We have to give credit to whom credit is due.

The present represents what it says, *pre-sent*? *Pre* of course is a prefix meaning something which existed before something else. Our all-knowing power has to be involved here because He is the only one who could have pre-existed. We should agree on this if man was created by some being of a greater power, right? That would mean that this creator existed before what He created, making Him pre-existing. Therefore, present is something we all have and were promised. We began at one stage and were allowed to move to another. We arrived at another stage, remembering where we used to be, not so that we could remain in the past but so that we could appreciate our present state.

To live in the past is to never develop or mature in a manner acceptable to succeed in the present. Also to live in the past is to never seek the intended good. The intended good in this case would be a change for the better. To never seek the intended good is to never find our beginning. This makes us a prime target for the intrusion of negative forces. We never change. We remain the same and our lives never reflect what the pre-sent says it should. We are alive in the present but we are living in the past.

We have no power and we cannot recognize the need of such because our past continues to be our obstacle. This higher power knows this but, because of our free will, patiently waits for our desire to have what He has already provided for us. Since He will never take our control from us, He waits for us to take control of what is trying to limit us. He gives us hints by waking us up everyday that we might realize another opportunity.

He also knows that our past can teach us about our present because upon it the value system was established, and because of it we found the need to seek what was already prepared. The enemy in our past is the opportunity to give up. But if we give up then we never receive what was pre-sent to us. The negative forces win and rule not just our past but also our wish for the present.

Traditional views limit progress toward the present and the future. Tradition should not be seen as a one-way ticket upon which the household of life is to function. Instead it should be seen as the foundation which the present is to be built, but not where it should be limited. Tradition is to follow what is right by becoming better at it each time. It is to learn from the past that we might be able to operate and function in the present. It is not to hold to the past that we might miss what was pre-sent.

The Past vs. the Present

To have created mankind, this almighty being had to live before it, which would make Him ruler of the past. To constantly intervene in our everyday lives would also make Him ruler of the present. To hear the voice of a lost soul would make Him alive and operable in the lives of the needful. To offer the same thing to everyone everywhere would make Him omnipresent and accessible for everyone, which would make Him the Almighty. Yes He exists and to deny His existence is to reject our own. Our past and our present give us a sense of being and awareness. Our life has substance because of our past experiences. If existing is living and having an affect on what we encounter, then what better description is there for such an awesome power. He is God. He rules and He reigns.

Chapter Nine

The Heart:
Mankind's Foundation of All Truths

We need it to function. We need it to access every commonality that's considered relevant in our lives. Without it we cannot breathe nor can the simple things provided for us be understood. It is important because upon it lies the emotional, intellectual, and the natural sensations, which we express as feelings. It is the centerpiece of what's so captivating about mankind because as often as it is spoken for, it still can never quite be explained. In it are the issues of life. Upon it hangs all the answers to one's own destiny. Through it lies every obstacle to be overcome and every challenge to be met for the strengthening of the soul.

It is so sensitive that the thought of sorrow brings tears to our eyes but it is so stubborn that we follow our own intuition even when we know it's wrong. It can be influenced but it cannot be moved. It acts as a receiver and a transmitter. The heart is known for its uniqueness in that life begins and ends with it; however, to open it up does not allow us to visit its incomparable design nor does it allow us to understand its higher connection.

There are no strings attached to it. There are no cable wires pulling on it to determine which actions should be considered appropriate. It seems to float within its created covering, receiving and interjecting back into life what it is allowed to. A higher influence, maybe; our own knowledge or intuition, I doubt it. Mankind is awesome in that he is able to move about the earth, pursuing the good of the land in what he prefers. But there are certain influences while he moves about, which stick out in his mind and cause him to decide to hear or reject what is trying to be spoken through his heart.

Communication through Our Eyes

Indeed, there are three modes of communication used to affect everything we do and every thought we have. There is first what we see through our eyes. Our eyes allow us to feel attracted to something. What we see opens up our preferences and what we are willing to settle for. It has a way of connecting with our inner soul to give us the right feeling to make a right choice.

This right choice often comes from our heart as it was created with a destination in mind to find its beginning state. Because it was naturally good, the heart knew what was acceptable and what was not. Although it was pre-existent in that we received it from our ultimate source, it was still subjected to something. While the origins of what used to be its perfect state became infected by wrong choices of mankind, the heart still yearns to have contact with its original source. This explains the peaceful feelings we encounter when our actions measure up with the feelings and expressions of our heart.

The eyes fill it with prejudices and preferences, trying to influence it in such a way that it holds inside all the natural good and reveals only what it sees. This happens when one begins his mode of sight from the wrong platform. Things should not be seen just from the eyes but from the heart. If the heart is subjected to its higher source, then the same values that exist with its source should be a measuring tool for how what is seen is to be perceived.

The eyes do not control the makeup of the heart but the heart determines the attractions of the eyes. What is seen as attractive or lustful is first subjected to whatever the heart is subjected to. If one allows the ponderances of the heart to be overlooked, then deception uses what the heart wishes to occupy. Then, what we normally would not consider acceptable, we find interest in, and curiosity leads us away from what we should follow, our heart.

How is that possible? Let's look at an example: a person who reads porno magazines and a person who sees a porno magazine but never reads it. The person who reads it has accepted within himself or herself, their heart, that it is OK to view such things for whatever reasons. They have compromised their avenue of communication. The person who sees the magazine while glancing in the magazine section has his or her heart convicted by such sights and, because of their discomfort, will look the other way. What they saw was challenged by their principle of preference as it relates to the perception of what is right and the effects it can have. The original good thoughts challenged the natural acceptable

The Essence of Life

ones and caused this person to make a choice. The choice depends on which force is given the most power.

To compromise one's heartfelt decisions is to allow anything. The problem with allowing anything is that, since the eyes serve as avenues of communication and influence, we can very well react based on false perceptions as opposed to what's right. This is not an attempt to explain every action of mankind, because in trying to do so I would become this higher source so many of us are trying to find, which of course is ridiculous. I only want to offer another view, which I believe to be an inspired one, that we may see what really matters and what doesn't.

The notion that what we put into the heart determines what we get out of it is true. We get paid for the amount of hours we work. If we work overtime we get paid for it and if we take days off without having the time to do so, we lose money and sometimes our job. Making good sound decisions is like working for our welfare. The more we coincide with our higher power, the better decisions we will make, limiting our mistakes or time off. The amount of peace we experience is our daily paycheck. The principles upon which we decide to live our lives are our base salary. We reap the benefits of knowing such a great power by resisting the opposing forces that wish to turn us away from the truth. We learn how to use our free will and not manipulate it.

Free will is something that should not be taken for granted because we are beginning to see that the choices we make hamper our lives, and there is no one else to blame but ourselves. Food is good and tasty but to prepare it with the wrong ingredients takes away its taste, and too much bad food can make us sick. The heart is a foundation of all the truths of mankind, but if filled with the wrong things contrary to what it knows to be right, then sicknesses occur and many times, death.

Do you not know that a person can die and still be walking around like we are? Death, a lot of the time, is associated with the physical loss of breath followed by a funeral service, but one can be dead on his feet. If the wrong influences take hold of our lives and separate us from our beginning source of power, then we are as good as dead because we are now living on our own and in our own way. This means we make all of our choices and what the eye sees the eye gets, even if it leads us to do something ungodly or unlawful. We are not subjected to anything, causing death of the soul. And death of the soul is like walking around in a circle, not knowing where to go or what to do, just following the scent of what we smell to be good. But be careful—some tasteful appetites can lead us to the garbage can.

The eyes—is it right to see what we want and to act upon it or is it the will of the heart to determine what is right to see? If this source of power is so great, is it possible that He would give us the right to see what we want, as often as we want, and then hold us accountable for how we act upon what we see? Could he have provided us with the ability to separate what is truly seen from how it should be perceived? I'm just throwing possibilities around, hoping to make sense out of this whole perception thing. I think that is what free will really is. It is having the opportunity to make a choice, whatever that choice may be, with the understanding that there will be a consequence with each choice we make.

So accountability is what our source of power uses to offset free will. He is saying, I have demonstrated what right is but you decide whether or not you think I'm right. He says, make a choice and follow it and be ready to deal with the outcome of your decision. Think about it—we could not be held accountable unless we were first given the opportunity to know the difference between right and wrong.

Hearing the Right Things

The second mode of communication is the ears. We generally respond to what we hear. Someone says hello and we respond by doing the same. We are insulted and some of us respond by insulting. Be it right or wrong, our responses are dictated by what we hear. What we hear helps us to process what we see. If someone is yelling at us, we hear the anger in their voice and we see from their expression that they are upset. We need to hear other people as well as our self conscious, or our heart. Although our heart is usually not heard audibly, we feel its desires and its efforts to lead us to a place of contentment and satisfaction.

What we hear is sent to our CPU unit upstairs in our brains to be checked out, to see what is good and what is junk. It is then determined what we allow to rest in the comforts of our heart. The hearing is so important here because, as the foundation of all truths, the last thing most of us want to hear is the truth. That is why at times we tune our inner voice out, our hearts, and become privy to our emotions. Although the truth walks beside us, we often times choose pleasure over truth. In a nutshell, we hear what we want to hear but we want the results of what we should have heard.

The ears work in harmony with the heart listening for all the positives and negatives which agree with the truth established in our heart. We all have principles and standards by which we choose to live. Some things we will compromise and some things we will not. The ears serve as the divider between these two choices. Some things we hear should enter one ear and go right out the other, but this only happens with those who refuse to compromise the beliefs they hold true in their hearts.

So now when common temptations make their way to our doorstep, because we hold true to our beliefs we can make sound decisions. I'm not saying we always do, I'm only saying we know what we should do. It is impossible to have a peaceful soul and an out-of-control heart or a peaceful heart and an out of control soul. The hearing acts as a desired craving. Our craving isn't satisfied until what we crave is in our hands. None of the many substitutes can ever give us what we really want so they never satisfy us.

The heart's desire is to receive what it needs to grow and live in peace, which it can receive from what is heard. Hearing the wrong things all the time makes it impossible for the intended good to prevail because what is desired is never realized. The intended good wishes to operate in all of mankind so that they might become all that they were created to be. We are not superficial beings designed to carry out tasks according to our own will. We are, however, designed to represent the intended good in whose image we were created.

Is it really so difficult to hear the right things? No, not if we pay attention to what our heart wants us to hear. We usually get out of life whatever we put into it. If we spend more time trying to regulate our heart condition, then we avoid all the mishaps and mess-ups attributed to our own counseling. This is, once again, not meant to demonstrate how bad humankind is but it is the opportunity to point us in the right direction that we might infect humankind with the intended good and not with the forces which oppose it.

To hear the heart we have to know it. To know it we have to spend time with it. To understand how a television set operates we look to the instruction guide that accompanies the purchase. If we have problems we check with customer service to find out the necessary procedures to get the results we want. If the problem persists then they usually direct us to the manufacturer. This is the starting point, from which the television set first became a thought. All of our answers are with the manufacturer. He is listening that he might inform us on what to do that our television set might function as it was designed to. The heart needs to hear from its manufacturer from time to time that we might know how to give it what it needs. But we are like most people with their television sets, working for hours and hours trying to figure out what the problem is. They never do, but end up pushing the wrong button or unhooking the wrong wire and breaking the television set.

This higher power could not have possibly made something without intervening from time to time. Although we have the right to move about and make choices on our own and hear what we wish as well as see all that opposes the truth, still we can never be completely free of our creator. We have to be able to hear Him that He might instruct us through the avenues of our hearts. The heart desires to hear the good because that is what ignites confidence, self-control, and belief. Since influences are so strong in today's society, we must all be careful of what we allow to enter into our CPUs, as what we hear may contradict what we need to hear, and the influence could be detrimental to our lives. Our actions should reflect what we believe in our heart and our heart should reflect what good things we have heard. Therefore, it must be able to unite with its original source in order to feel comfortable and peaceful. Then when we look to our heart for answers, we are not so surprised when it reveals the truth.

Speaking the Truth

The third mode of communication is that of the mouth. The mouth usually speaks what was allowed to enter into the heart. After the eyes have viewed what they find to be interesting, the mind provides a sort of subjective bridge upon which the pros and the cons are weighed. Whatever was heard through the ears about this particular subject will now influence the thoughts about the situation. If negative thoughts take over, that is what the heart receives. When an opportunity comes for a reply, the mouth will speak whatever was allowed in the heart.

We lift people up and we tear people down with our mouths. Just as quickly as we give you a reason to smile, in the same breath we can make you cry. The mouth can sing praises to whatever it chooses but it can only reveal what is in the heart. This almighty power could not expect us, as His offspring, to hold the jewels of communication inside without expressing ourselves in some way. We make gestures with our hands and expressions with our face, but the mouth makes our feelings clear. With the mouth we can even attest or detest the existence of a higher power. Some say we should always be able to say what we feel but if our actions should always reflect the intended good, then what we say should always be the truth.

This is not to say we should never express a negative thought but we should be careful how we express it so that its main purpose reflects the intended good and not just how we feel. I may not at times want others to see the reflection of a greater connection between my source and me, but because my heart is subjected to this higher power, all the words my mouth speaks have to be in line with the same power source. If we only expressed our feelings, we would always have to feel great in order to say what we should, and we would suffer when the time comes to do what is right. This higher good wants us to express ourselves all the time. The more we express ourselves, the more we believe in what we are proclaiming. Our heart can then convict us of our own thoughts, which causes us to become curious about another way. This causes us to seek something higher that we might have peace with what we feel.

None of us wants to fail. None of us wants to intentionally do wrong but we do greatly err when we use what was supposed to be positive for the negative. In doing so we no longer hear what we should hear and the opposing forces influence us and cause us to go in another direction. We begin to say all kinds of things only to realize that we are speaking without listening to our hearts.

The mouth is a powerful source of communication. With it we represent all that we feel and because of it our actions are weighed. There must be a force which tries to impose upon us the intended good because, even when our feelings require of us one mode of response, we are always presented with an alternative, which usually reflects the characteristic of our higher source. The choice is ours to make. However, if our mouths speak what our emotions feel then our words can haunt us. We say sticks and stones can break our bones but words can never hurt us. This would be so nice if it were true. The only problem is that most of the time our feelings get hurt, not from a stick or a stone, but from the mouth of someone who delivered the words which bruised our soul. Sticks and stones bruise the outward body parts but they can never hurt the soul. The words, however, can be left to ponder within the heart, causing internal pain and of course making it more difficult to act upon the intended good of the heart.

What a dilemma—or is it? Think about it. This positive force has to allow the negative to exist with the positive so that a choice can be formed and the heart can be influenced in one way or the other. It is a way of challenging the will to find what's right. This is done by speaking what is true, which first begins with what is received in the heart. What is the purpose of this all-knowing source if He knows the end of a thing and yet sits back and watches the outcome, and then holds us accountable for the end result?

The Heart: Mankind's Foundation of All Truths

If our parents had given us everything we asked for, we would never know what it is to need. If we were never sad, we would never be able to appreciate the happy times. Trust would be non-existent because it would not be necessary. Faith would be a joke because what we see is what we would expect to receive. If this force would not allow us to operate under our own discovery, then the reins of the heart would not be able to be tried. Our free will would be an option, just as surround sound is the construction of our homes. It would be useless to expect any other action from us if He made us do what He wanted us to do.

Before I contradict myself, let's pay attention to the plan and purpose of this powerful force. Any creator of anything knows the intended purpose for which it was created. The strategy is to implement the intended purpose within what was created without taking away from what was made. Even though things malfunction after creation, we never tear them down but we find a way within what we made to get the intended result. Although malfunctions sometimes damage the created thing in the eyes of its creator, it still has potential to be what it was supposed to be.

Free will is the greatest characteristic of freedom any of us can ever exercise. Our actions cannot and should not be forced or predetermined by anyone; however, this higher power allows us as His created people to decide what we like and dislike, and where we want to go and what we wish to accomplish in our short lives. This force is operative in every decision we make. He is there in every situation of our lives. Sometimes He manifests Himself in some form or another and other times He waits to be invited to manifest Himself in our lives. He hopes that our curiosities will lead us to a point of influence, where we will constantly use His awesome power as a measuring tool for our lives and not our lives as measuring tools for His power.

Why doesn't He just tell us if He really does have interest in our well-being and happiness? When was the last time we listened to our heart? Who knows, that feeling we had before we were married maybe was not the human interpretation of "cold feet," but was the voice of our source telling us he or she just wasn't the one. But because of our own evaluation of what meets our standards, we went through with it and now we can't figure out why things are the way they are. One thing is clear to us—we should have listened to our heart and not our specific preferences.

How about when our friends pressured us into taking our first drink or experimenting with drugs. There was a nervousness within us that made us uncomfortable and there was a feeling of inadequacy while being lost in the world of temptation. Could this have been our guidance from within and above? Could this force have been trying to make contact with us through what possessed the answers to all our questions, the heart?

What about the types of friends we continue to associate with, knowing we have nothing in common. Every time we are around them we feel sick and wish we had the power to leave because our heart yearns and aches when we try to fit into a group that is just not our kind. But we continue trying to fit a square peg into a round hole. Is He speaking to us or are we just not listening?

What about the material things we purchase which go beyond what we are able to afford, deepening our debt and the sacrifices we are willing to make becoming greater burdens. We work ourselves to the bone just trying to keep up with our payments and our friends. Is He talking to us in some kind of way or are we just not listening?

Should He show up in some great form just to tell us what to do? He won't because He respects our free will even when it contradicts what dwells in our hearts. And just like

The Heart: Mankind's Foundation of All Truths

all other forces that try to influence the heart, our source wants us to allow Him to dwell in our hearts that we might reflect the beauty that life entails. These other forces have no right to try to possess what they didn't create but this creator of mankind has the right to protect what He made that they may become what He intended them to be. If love is the highest expression of the most intimate feeling then what greater example do we have than our source continuing to love what He created although at times it contradicts itself.

Once again the main question is, does this higher power rule the reigns of the center of existence, the heart? Yes He does. He instructs what He created that the reflection of the intended good can clearly be seen. Otherwise, how would mankind even know what is right if his creator didn't first put into him what should come out of him.

Chapter Ten

The Bible

The question of the Bible's origination and the actual inspirational views given to a select few writers form the uncertainties associated with this book of truth. This book is a compilation of what we all need and require in order to trust and believe. It contains facts and acts which represent the acclaimed power given to it. Should such a higher force seek to reveal Himself in an acceptable form to His creation or should His creation seek the form in which He chooses to reveal Himself? We as humans demonstrate our ignorance in demanding from a higher source an acceptable explanation for His actions, that we might believe that He is who He says He is. This is a backwards view that drastically needs to be changed that we might operate in the purpose for which we were created and bear witness of the existence of the truth.

It is no strange thing that the Bible is questioned and at times misrepresented and misunderstood. However, our mode of reception doesn't lie in the logical interpretations of the learned, but it is revealed to each of us based on our search and belief in the truth. We as human beings always base the fact of the existence of a higher power on our personal dilemmas or the experiences we encounter. Therefore, we think about the goodness of a higher power only when something good happens to us. We question the actions or the power of this higher being when we experience things we feel to be contrary to what is considered good. We form questions which hinder our belief in the truth instead of allowing our curiosities to become our reasons to search for such a being.

Human beings wish to know all they think is necessary to believe that a higher power exists, only to find that He can't be scientifically defined. He is, however, scientifically proven by the very facts upon which the theories of the universe are based. The cause and effect theory denotes the beginning of a greater force. The tracing of human history or life in any form denotes the beginning of an existing force. The different elements and chemical bonds that make up our world today attest to the fact that there was a well-thought-out plan before anything ever existed. The anthropology of mankind defines itself within the realms of what it considers good or bad acknowledging the fact that it came from an all-knowing source of power.

This higher source of existence cannot be explained by His creation but He can only be trusted by it. He should be respected and accepted without trying to be placed in the limited space of human understanding. He should be left to explain Himself and why He chooses to exist the way He does and why He wishes to reveal Himself the way He does. And just because the curiosity of the human soul desires answers to questions, which will serve as the opportunity to ask more questions, this should not be a reason to exert non-belief.

In realizing the wish of the heart of mankind to connect with its original source, this source provides a way to interject His truths into what He made, that He might not only be heard but that He may be seen. What do you mean, *seen*? We know that this force is invisible and whether we are devout followers of the faith or not, He doesn't walk the earth today. This question and answer usually follows such statements relative to the visualization of such a higher power in the confinements of humanity today. True, the force of today is invisible, but not unforeseeable. He reveals the truth of His words through the hearts of the people today. So, although we can't physically see a bodily shape that can be deemed the Almighty, we can see the very way in which each of us lives our lives. Our actions do speak louder than our words because it's our actions that state our connection with such a divine force. To argue the relativity of the Bible is to search for the truth in what is being revealed. If we all embrace the truths of this divine inspirational compilation, then maybe what we denounce as myths, we could cling to as our source of power.

Beginning Instructions

The Bible is something that will continue to be debated because it poses an obstacle to those who choose to disregard it. It withstands being questioned or theologically evaluated as the answer to all walks of life because of its inspired origination. Contrary to ongoing debates about the authenticity of the writings, each viewpoint arrives at the same ending of truth, that such an awesome power exists and still moves within mankind today.

The people upon whom this source revealed Himself relayed the message first given to them. They served the same purpose a sister or brother serves today. Our mothers and fathers delegate and deliver messages through our siblings. The fact that our mother or father didn't speak directly to us doesn't mean that they didn't speak the message relayed to us. The fact that Mom said or Dad said is enough to cause us to move with obedience, even though we have our own opinion. The prophets delivered the very words of the Almighty. They only spoke as they were moved by the spirit of a higher being. It should be enough for us to follow the written words of a divine ruler instead of rejecting our source by questioning His authenticity.

The Bible is an instruction guide seen through the eyes of this great being as the platform and blueprint upon which life is to be constructed. It deals with every issue relative to mankind and has to be diligently sought after in order to have a changing effect upon one's life. In fact, it is such an instruction guide that BIBLE actually stands for Beginning Instructions Before Leaving Earth. Interesting huh? I thought so too. Beginning instructions before leaving earth. This attests to the fact that mankind had a purpose before life was even given to him. He was created with his beginning and ending within himself, and only his creator knows his beginning and his ending.

Beginning instructions means that before our actions could be weighed, we would have to have been given the proper instructions as to how we should react and conduct ourselves relative to every situation. Right was known before wrong was discovered. This almighty instruction giver was what right represented, and He defined righteousness through His revelational words that make up the Bible. As a higher power, it was His duty to provide the answers to the challenges mankind would face so that he would be held accountable for his choices.

He inspired the visible by the invisible so that He could become the walking word of life, clearly seen by those who would question His existence. He wants us to read about His character and trust in the truths that are revealed throughout the generations of the world so that we might accept and embrace the meaning of life. Therefore, a guide would be necessary to remind and constantly instruct, as well as strengthen what He created so that the intended good could be realized. Beginning instructions before means that obviously there was some kind of preparation in the making. The livelihood of our good nature is understood by our relationship with our beginning source. To not seek His knowledge through the written words of His revelation is to openly deny our original connection.

The Bible is our source of revelation from Him who chooses to make Himself known in a special but distinct way. Sometimes we become angry or unconvinced because someone chooses another method, other than the one we have in mind, to defend themselves or explain themselves. I have the right to tell you about as much of my life as I wish. It doesn't mean I'm distant or uncommunicative, it just means I am the determinant factor as to how much of my life I will reveal. Our source chose people and, just to remind us daily, He wrote the very inspirational words in a book, the Bible, so that we could hear a thing and then have something to compare it to, and ultimately making our own decisions.

There will always be the human dilemma as to the extent of the truth that comes from the human being. There will always be questions as to life in general. Personally, I think we concern ourselves with minor issues too much, which in turn takes our focus off finding the truth. Does it really matter why this higher being chose the men of that day instead of the preferred kings and queens or any other person of renown? Is it really that difficult to understand that even our theological study only gives us a glimpse of what is in store for those who question and seek and receive and believe the truth about our greater source? I cannot generalize our higher connection and I think I do Him an injustice if I try to do so. However, I have a question each of us can ponder—do you remember being born and can you pinpoint the day you will die? There is a greater force that begins a thing and finishes it at the same time. The Bible never gives the answers to all of our sometimes profound inquiries but it does provide a hope and a security that is unmatched when it is believed.

If you have never studied the Bible intensely, try it and then attempt to apply some of the principles to your life. Then before you conclude that this stuff is for the birds, look at your life in retrospect and pinpoint when a change started to take place. I will even say that if you can read the Bible with no effect on your life, then the words I'm speaking are not inspired but are my own and please send me your address and I will gladly send you a refund for the purchase of this book.. I guarantee your vision will change. I guarantee your outlook will be different from before. I even guarantee that you will begin to discover things about yourself that you never knew existed.

Instead of leaving the human dilemma to the imagination of the lost, this force provides His creation with a guide, the Bible, which serves as the visible personhood of our higher being. The Bible is the reason why we should seek to find our original place in this infinite being, because when we seek to know this power through His inspired words, we connect with the beginning of all things. Would scholars seek

The Bible

to dissect such a power source if it allowed amendments to the rule? How about if the source of power would not ever punish or allow consequences from one's actions, would mankind have a problem with such a power? I think not because, although we are originally good, we as humankind have fallen from our original state. We have to be led back by our instruction guide. The Bible is always questioned because it places limitations on our actions, forcing us to make a choice. This higher power chooses to reveal Himself through an inspired book provided for creation, with the opportunity to use it or despise it. One thing is for sure, those who follow it cannot deny it, and those who seek this power through His word always find Him and they are never the same afterward.

To subject this book to human knowledge is not reasonable because it was not written from the human mind. To disallow the effect of this book because of questions as to the state of mind of the writers is to think that this source of power is incapable of explaining Himself. To derive from this book negative excuses as to why He doesn't exist is to look in the mirror and say, I created all that I see. Anything good is always detested because it is seen as being different. It is seen in a strange light. It places fear in the pathway of all those who wish to become stumbling blocks in front of it. This book can continue to be questioned but it will never be disproved. It can continue to be challenged but it will never be defeated, as it contains the oracles of life. It can constantly be tested as it pertains to everyday living but each of us, whether we agree or disagree, will always be walking testimonies each day we wake up. This force wakes us up everyday with the hope that if we believe, we might proclaim our belief and if we don't that the truth might be revealed to us that day.

Did God actually inspire men to write such things? Did He take it upon Himself to use what men could see to reveal

Himself? Could He possibly have been thinking clearly to try to trick us into thinking that He actually exists? First of all, this force is God because He is the source of knowledge. He is also greater than any other limited characteristic of creation. He used what He created to be seen within mankind. If we represent such a character then our actions should flow with that of the image we emulate.

    Is His existence really a trick? Deceivers have to trick us because they have to overcome the truth, which exists in us. This great force could not trick Himself because, first, He didn't have to, if the Bible stresses free will. Second, He doesn't trick what He created because that would make him a lie, if creation was to reveal His character. Is the Bible the authentic truth from God revealed through human beings to instruct what He created? Yes it is, because it explains the foundation of all truths as they are seen through the heart. Each word reflects His character that we, as His people, might get to know Him intimately, establishing faith in what we cannot see and the hope to trust in our great creator.

Chapter Eleven

Prosperity:
The Right to Succeed

Can we give anyone anything without possessing it first? From an extra pair of shoes to a few dollars for a hot meal, could any of us provide such necessities without possessing the means to fulfill such needs? Thoughts are wonderful and wishes to help the needy are admirable, but without the means to do so they are just empty dreams with hopeful goals.

There is a beginning for all things. And all things derive their meaning in life from their beginning source. People can't advise others relative to their situation without first understanding what their problem is. The beginning of all things cannot infiltrate the lives of those who need Him until they realize the source of beginnings is also the answer to all dilemmas.

Even though each of us has the right to succeed, we often fail because we forget to prioritize the most meaningful things in our lives. Therefore, we define success by what we possess and not by the content of our character. We define success by who we feel like we are and not by a connection with a greater source. After all, it is easier this way because the reflection of material wealth can be seen whereas the source of all power cannot. We dealt with the reflection of the true image in the previous chapters and concluded that we reflect what we are close to.

We reflect the image of our parents because many of us are close to our parents. They have taught us certain values in life to maintain for our own good, and we become the finished products of obedience by representing what they instilled in our hearts. We all would like to own something of value in our lifetime, if for nothing else, to be able to pass them on to our children and grandchildren that it might reflect a part of us, but many of us would love to have good things spoken about us more than just what we possessed.

Prosperity is not just seen in the outward appearance of the abundance of things. Prosperity is measured in two ways: the ways of society and the divine intervention from a greater source. One starts from the outside in whereas the other builds from the inside out. One can change the hearts of others and the other can ruin the hearts of others by reflecting only abundance and not substance. Prosperity is not negative because it is a good thing but it becomes our worst nightmare when we believe that it is all that matters. It becomes an avenue for negative forces, setting the stage for jealousy, envy, and hate. It does it because we allow it to. It can become contagious for generations to come unless we seek prosperity from our known source of power.

We must instill in our children the will to prosper and the meaning of a divine connection because they will be a reflection of our pursuit of prosperity. If we seek it at all cost, sacrificing all to attain it, so will they. It will become the cornerstone of what they will feel is necessary in order to be accepted in life. They will conform to all rules instead of being transformed by the truth. Our source is a part of us and we are a part of Him and this alone makes us prosperous. He is beautiful because He reflects only the best of things. He is demanding because He challenges us to draw closer to Him everyday in everyway. This great image is real, for we see Him around us everyday. To reflect His image through material gain is icing on the cake. Notice the icing on the cake just adds to the taste of the cake but it doesn't take away from the fact that the cake is still tasty and good even without the icing.

Don't be mistaken, to possess is to distribute and if you seek to possess a lot, be ready to give even more. But if you don't have a lot from a material standpoint don't be dismayed. Just be content with your current state and continue to seek Him who possesses all things. You are prosperous, you are a jewel in the making, and when your time comes, people won't just call you prosperous but they will call you blessed.

Prosperity Determined by the Foundation

Could the image of the great ones that we embrace so willingly be the manifestation of a greater force? Could the best of all things reveal Himself from time to time through human beings of whom we grow to admire? Could He just be revealing Himself through a common interest that He might hold our attention, and for our sakes that we might draw closer to Him because of what we see? This great image

The Essence of Life

that strives with each of us desires to have us become all that we should. He does not desire that we have everything we want because some of us may not want Him after we get from Him all that we wish.

All of these are questions which none of us have the answers to. We don't, not because we cannot find a logical way to explain the content of a powerful source, but because we depend on a greater force to reveal Himself in a personal way to each living being. What do you mean? I mean that there are certain levels of expectations, which drive each of us to the maximum throughout our daily lives. Our expectations are seen in our quest to earn as much money as possible or to marry the most beautiful person on the planet. We see glimpses of the best of things when we see those who drive the best cars and those who live in the best of houses. This makes us associate prosperity with the material.

Prosperity is not something that should be viewed as a negative by those who are not as fortunate but it should be seen as a reflection of the possibility and opportunity each of us has. Every house might not contain the same square footage; however, it is a possession and shouldn't be compared to the expectations of others. Every car is of a different value but all are personal possessions and should be seen as such. We reflect the prosperity we seek. To not have a material reflection doesn't mean we are not prosperous and to have everything the world dreams of doesn't make us prosperous.

Prosperity is determined by the foundation upon which we define our lives. In order to define our lives, our foundation has to be solid and immovable. It has to be deeply rooted in what matters. Material possessions don't really matter. Actually, they are only small bits of gratification, distributed to us for our own personal enjoyment, if our principles of life are correctly prioritized.

Prosperity Not Limited to an Elite Group

The next question is, where do the poor and less fortunate fit into this lopsided world? There will always be people who need help. Maybe those who have the means to do so were trusted with such gifts to support the needs of others while satisfying themselves. If every one of our actions are weighed and challenged by the law of a greater force, then surely our destinies are intertwined so that the good news might reach those who are looking for it in a variety of ways.

Those who reflect what others seek should influence admirers by acknowledging the source of their accomplishments. This gives the less fortunate hope and the would-be greats the understanding of a greater force. The negative force of jealousy should never be allowed to deprive us of the belief that prosperity is not limited or confined to some people of an elite group. It involves everyone from all backgrounds to join in one vision of a prosperous future for all people. After all, it is our right to pursue prosperity and to embrace it, but not before we develop it and receive it from Him who possesses it. This force wants to change the feeling of jealousy into one of appreciation so that everyone can believe that they truly have the right to succeed and the right to have the things that reflect success.

This is not to say that our desire to possess should outweigh our desire to know our creator because if such a thing happens, we replace what is true and eternal with that which is temporal and external. Anything external affects those who see us and causes them to form a false opinion of what we have and what we reflect. Prosperity looks like it's our friend but we haven't even met him. We become imitators instead of participators. We begin to misrepresent and give all the false implications that define a lie. The things which are true are the things that last. The things we reflect upon are the things we hold true in our heart. Things change but the positive forces never change because they are forever trying to prepare us for what we so diligently seek—prosperity.

Priority Is the Road to Prosperity

Prosperity is something promised to us because it represents our desires after we have acknowledged our original state of existence. I said *after we have acknowledged our original state of existence* because priority is the road to prosperity. Without the right perspective and principles, prosperity will always live around the corner from each of us. Most of us are not millionaires because we don't know how to be dollaraires yet. We do not manage our current state but seek a more prosperous one. Prosperity is ours to have but it is also ours to lose.

Life is linked closely to maturity. Maturity comes with time and the more time passes, the wiser we become because we learn what's important and what's not. It happens in stages just like most of our childhood growth spurts. None of us could pass from one stage to the next without understanding the previous stage first.

To experience prosperity we have to know who represents prosperity. I mean we have to know Him just like we know our wives or girlfriends. We have to put forth the effort to cultivate a relationship with such a force just as we wish to improve our golf game or put ourselves in position for promotions. We have to seek Him with the diligence of a lion preparing to attack its prey.

We can only understand how to succeed by following and then leading others. But before we can lead we have to follow. Success involves submission. To submit is to acknowledge the all-knowing ability of another. As our search for what matters changes, we as human beings have to redirect our search. The search can no longer lie in the external self-indulgences of what makes us feel superior or in control. The search can no longer dwell in the ambition to rule the world from an authoritative position, nor can the search exist in the opportunity to create an image in the minds of our peers that will cause them to form a positive opinion about us. But the search would have to begin from within. It would have to begin with Him who has the power to direct and to correct. The search would have to be for what matters the most and not just for what reflects the best of things. The first would have to be developed before the second could be established. The multitude of possessions can contain a graveyard full of tombstones because trust would become an object and not the defining characteristic of Him who desires each of our souls.

A divine connection produces an inner bond forming the perfect foundation that leads to a lifelong dream of prosperity. But we have to know this source intimately, emotionally, and intellectually. This requires time just as any relationship does. We shouldn't try to go to bed with someone we just met for the first time because obviously we don't know them well enough. We need time to figure out if what they want is what we have to give and vice versa. The same principles apply here. This almighty force needs to trust us with the divine riches that feed and nourish the soul, which develops and cultivates our relationship with Him. To give us something we may not be capable of handling is to give us too much too soon, just like sleeping with someone you just met—only to realize later that you have no interest in him or her at all.

Seek the higher good because it brings with it the inner security and peace which nothing external can provide, but don't deceive yourself by only seeking His face for your own personal gain. Listen to your soulish man, your heart, and not the world around you because if you haven't recognized it already, society does not have the same understanding of success as this incomparable source.

True Success

Society teaches us to follow our own rules, even if it means breaking the laws of the land and compromising our personal values. It teaches us to win at all cost. It teaches us that the strong survive and the weak become the servants to those who rule. Those who rule are those who have acquired a bundle of possessions. He who succeeds by the regulated rules of society fails to realize that such cases cause us to forget what we need to survive. We use wealth as the main example of success because it makes us look like we represent something greater. This force, which watches over us, supplies us and instructs us in the way we should go, so that we don't lose what we find and don't misunderstand what true success means.

We are all connected to this higher source of power and not even our free will can separate His intended wishes for us. But there are stipulations which must be satisfied before we can even become representatives in the area of prosperity for such a force. We have to find our beginning, searching for the face of Him who represents all things. We know this force exists because we would not have these intuitive feelings if it were not for such a force. We contain all that we seek. In our hearts lies the essence of life, from strength and faith to joy and prosperity. It is in us but we have to find it by seeking Him who wishes to possess our hearts. To find such a force opens the door for our wishes to become reality. To deny such a force the authority to rule closes the door of prosperity in our lives.

Deception then takes over and begins to play tricks on our minds, making us think that those who have more than we do, think they are better than we are. The truth is, that person has found the force which desired them and they have let Him rule their lives. We cannot quite understand because one of the stipulations was to sacrifice some of our concerns and wishes that this force might reveal Himself through us in His way. We would have to give our heart to a force we cannot see, which would require us to have faith. Faith warrants prosperity because it acknowledges the fact that such a force exists. This force, which wishes to dwell in each of us openly, not just in our homes or in our churches, would have no choice but to reveal Himself to us if we let Him, or else He would run the risk of becoming a liar. Lying is a negative quality, which cannot exist with such a force if we as mankind are to represent only the truth. Therefore, the words of this force words have to be true if He is not to contradict Himself.

So is prosperity measured by what we have? By society's standards, yes. But that force which first gave man the opportunity to rule and follow Him in such a way that he would always succeed shows us that a man's success is not measured by the things he possesses. The less fortunate or even the poor, for example, are some of the most secure and happy people we could ever meet. Because they live where they live, does this mean they are not successful? Is having all our needs met without having the abundance of leftovers mean we are not prosperous? This higher power would have to disagree because the very image in which we were created was self-sufficient and if we wanted more, we would have to seek the face of Him who had it.

I will lend my opinion here. I think that this force would have us represent Him in the best of ways with the best of things. I think just as some foods affect people differently so does prosperity when it comes to monetary gain. If such a force could foresee the future of all things then surely

He could see who could and who couldn't handle all that they thought they could. So does He withhold prosperity from some? Just as a person with a weight problem has to refrain from unacceptable cravings so do those who wish to have things for the wrong reasons. He doesn't withhold anything from anyone. He is a provider not a withholder; therefore we limit and withhold the true things from ourselves when we openly refuse to abide by the rules of Him who reigns. Surely there are those who cheat to gain and manipulate to prevail but don't be mistaken, this is not success, this is a crime and an assault upon their own soul.

Once again, the question remains, is this positive force God? I should say so if with Him lies the best of all things and our predestined future, which no one else can decide nor dictate to us. The beginning starts with Him, and it will end with Him whether we choose to accept it or argue it until it happens. The very characteristics we consider to be good have stemmed from our source of power. He is God and to deny him the glory as such is to wipe away our lives from existence as the rain is washed from our windshield on a rainy day. Ask yourself, your soul, if it believes and when you receive your answer, follow it and hold to it, for upon it is your way out and your way in.

Chapter Twelve

The Mind:
The Acknowledgment of Good and Evil

The essence of a thought is the action displayed because of the thought. This is no new thing—our actions are dictated by what we think. The CPU of a computer can make decisions based on the input given to it. It knows the wrong choices because it has been given the right ones and it can always make the right choice, regardless of the difficulty of the problem. Our lives as human beings should mean enough to us that we shouldn't neglect our source of power, which serves as our strength and our outlook in life. We have been given the answers by which we are to make decisions. We have been given example after example that we might follow that which follows the good, so we might not come short of our predestinated place.

Before we can make a decision, we have to think about the choices presented to us. We have to realize the consequences of our choices. Some decisions we make will affect the rest of our lives and some decisions we make could possibly end our lives. We have to subject our thoughts to something greater. We have to evaluate our options very carefully because confusion is sometimes the result of deception and the will to not be subjected to a greater source.

This process of the mind is where the frustrations of life seem to overtake us when we can't seem to make sense out of what we think. The mind is the pathway to belief. It is where we accept deception or embrace the truth. It is where we choose to ignore the common bad and cling to a different source. The mind is the tell-all part of our souls. After all, it is the house of our souls. Things and situations are weighed here. Choices live here and the common good is known here because the mind is in this realm where the battle of the good vs. evil takes place. The common good is known here because it is entrusted with the ability to decide which course to take. Deception and mind boggling temptations wish to be found here because as a man thinketh so is he; therefore, whatever is allowed to live here becomes a characteristic of one's personality.

This is true because of the image in which mankind came into being. This almighty source provided us with the ability to think for ourselves, to decide for ourselves, and more importantly to believe for ourselves. Peer pressure and group influence here are just excuses for not making our own decisions. Indeed, those we spend quality time with will affect us but an influence is not an obligation, but a choice. If it isn't then free will is a contradiction of mankind. We all decide for ourselves or should I say have the power to decide for ourselves. This is not the choice of others and most of the

The Mind: The Acknowledgment of Good and Evil

time it is not the most popular decision to make but it is the result of a choice which defines our character.

In the mind there are a million and one choices and options per minute. The mind is the battlefield of human existence but it is also the strength of the soul. We resist the evil and cling to the good here. We develop justifications here that meet our own personal objectives. We can understand the motto "a mind is a terrible thing to waste," because if we misuse our mind, we reflect our insecurities and if it gains strength from its higher source, then we engage in suitable activities which exemplify the truth and give us peace.

Our Most Powerful Attribute

This great image in which we are created loaned us His good traits; therefore, when we locate and receive in our minds these naturally uncommon characteristics but spiritually necessary aspects, we open our hearts to a new world. We are now getting in touch with our beginning source and our lives begin to change because in seeking the answers to such curiosities we find the truth—we find ourselves.

The mind is the most powerful attribute we have because upon it hangs all the equipment needed to fulfill a dream or even to fantasize about the future. It contains the truths of mankind. We now begin to understand our divine purpose here on earth. We process our emotions in the mind, and we understand the simple uses of our senses. We determine what we like and dislike based on the choices we make in our minds. Just as judgments are created here, so are our successes. Notions like, be all you can be, never stop believing in yourself, and the sky is the limit are all sayings which deal with the mind. Our self-esteem is generated by what we allow ourselves to think. Sometimes thoughts enter our minds that we never thought about, only to be challenged by what we believe. We have the ability to affect our personal outcomes and we create the necessary options to continue down the right path or to detour our journey.

The mind is full of challenges and options that can be controlled by what we kick out and what we hold on to. Our self-confidence dwells in our minds. This is an important area for each of us because deception can steal away our self-confidence, which affects our self-esteem. I said all of that to say this: to take advantage of an opportunity, we have to decide to. To follow anything, we once again have to decide to. Although our beliefs are affected by unanswered questions, the mind is constantly struggling with the knowledge of good and evil. These two are constantly trying to replace one another, the one for the good and the other for the lustful bad.

The Mind As a Dictator

The most satisfying things are those which are accepted as being true, not those which are decided to be true, with human logic replacing divine truth. Anything that is rationalized is compromised, which makes it incomplete. The mind builds our soul and strengthens it. It purifies it because we now see and operate in a new light. No one can figure it out because our view is not obstructed anymore but constructed upon a sure foundation. The mind opens our heart up to the truth. It fills it or pollutes it. It builds it up or tears it down. It allows the structures of divine truth to reign and rule one's actions. It establishes a connection with its original source. It thrives on the union with such power because only then can it fulfill the desires of the heart.

The desires of the heart have to be a reflection of what's decided in the mind. Belief in a greater source provides for us the strength to break through barriers and overcome all obstacles, beyond our human capability. Some people term

The Mind: The Acknowledgment of Good and Evil

such things as miracles and others hallucinations but to those who accept the divine intervention of a greater source, we call it the power of God. To face the truth is to realize that we need Him who defines the truth. This is an important aspect to realize because in doing so we become dependent upon our greater source of power. We become able to differentiate between what thoughts we should allow to materialize and those we should destroy.

The intrusion of such a powerful source commands the challenge of an opposing force. Where else would such an opposing force attack besides the battlefield of the human decision making device—the mind. Our enemy desires to play mind games relative to our situations so that what is good doesn't appear that way, and what is to be expected can't even be seen. Instead of being optimistic we become pessimistic. Instead of challenging the issues by seeking the source of power, we accept whatever makes sense, trying to make the illogical logically understandable.

Remember, the mind doesn't want to fit in with anything; however, it does want to cling to what it knows to be the common good. That is where it finds peace and rest for the soul. This is where our perspective is visualized. The mind forms our priorities because here we consider the most important things in our lives. Just as man is a two-fold being, a human being and a spiritual being, he also possesses three intricate pieces, which make up his character—the mind, the heart, and the soul. These three have to agree and function in one accord or else the mind is defeated. Once again, I do not wish to define the problems of mankind but I do wish to say here that if our mind is infected with opposing thoughts relative to the common good then our heart will fail us because it will not recognize the correct way to function. It then begins to operate on emotional highs, always hearing but never able to understand.

The mind is very important because here we build our personal foundations, from our aspirations to be great to our wish for religious security. We allow deceptive forces to constantly cause division and stereotyping, as well as envying and hatred. The mind delivers to the heart and the heart, when it is full, will speak whatever we have allowed it to eat. If we have allowed it to receive honesty then it will speak honesty. The mind functions as a dictatorship. It dictates the actions to the other pieces because of what it receives.

The Choice Is Ours

Many of us look to the statistical columns to analyze the different theories as to what makes bad people bad and the seemingly good people good. We talk about everything from one's background to their upbringing to the types of groups they are affected by and even the cause of low self-esteem. We look for reasons to explain the negative reactions of such cases but we never speak about where it all began. We never talk about the spiritual background of a person unless he or she is a minister of some sort, because we do not want to be faced with having to confront a higher source.

First, because we can't explain Him. We will never be able to explain such a source of power but we will always be aware of His presence. His shadow is an everlasting engraving in our minds. Whether we choose to utilize His existence or constantly challenge His validity, it will never change this one fact: we all are aware of a higher source of power—we just don't accept it as we should. Those who do accept it are seen and pointed out as being different or attempting to emulate something, which can't be understood.

Our energy should be spent subjecting the thoughts, which enter our minds, to a power source, which is able to overcome them. We should seek to understand the difference

The Mind: The Acknowledgment of Good and Evil

between the forces, which affect us all, in one way or another. To know oneself is to be in control of our minds. The mind is the cornerstone of the knowledge of good and evil because it is there that we decide which forces will rule. The bad thoughts or good thoughts do not become sin or rewardable until they are put into action. Therefore, forces do not control us but we control them. A snowball only becomes bigger if it's allowed to roll and consume more snow. The principal of negativity is the same—it grows and sooner or later it becomes so big that we can't see the forest for the trees. There is a whole world on the other side but we never know it because we can't see it.

The mind is our mode of survival. It's our hidden strength when all else fails. It is so because this is where we acknowledge our source of power. Our heart is moved and we all feel deeply about certain things, of which our gut relays a sure message, but it is in the mind where we are at the crossroads. Our hidden voice seems to speak to our minds. It seems to find a way of revealing Itself to those who want to hear from It. We are not robots who only move about after we have been programmed. But we have our own minds, which are constantly under attack.

We may argue regarding the existence of such a force and His reasons for doing what He does, but can we really argue with the good that we see? I think not because the good be it nature, technology or even the common consideration for others is all good. These areas are very good. They cannot be matched. They can only be admired and administered. Even the very things we wish to imitate are the very images transpired from the thoughts of our minds. This is why we have to protect what we need to survive.

We have to protect our minds from the drug-infested forces, which wish to hamper our progress and deny the ability to believe and trust in a higher source. We have to protect what we should control by allowing its inventor to dwell in what He made. To live life in our own way could be life threatening because what we see is limited and it unfolds as we go about our courses in life. To allow such a higher power the opportunity to dwell in the comforts of what He knows to be the pathway to eternity is to be led by a force that sees the entirety of a thing. He can't let us down although He can allow us to be tried for the strengthening of the soul and the increasing of faith and trust in Him.

The choice is ours. People are going to have an opinion about us even if we never open our mouths, but so will our maker. The mind is a terrible thing to waste but so is an opportunity to get to know the greatest source of power to ever exist. Is He God? What do you think? The answer lies in your mind and it's your decision and yours alone. It doesn't lie in your big house or your luxury auto. The answer is one that is not a reflection of what you humanly can possess—it lies in your mind. It doesn't matter how much money you make, which is not a bad thing, but we all regardless of our situations will have to make the ultimate decision as to what we believe.

We are in the mind and the result of what we think lies in what decisions we make in our minds. Our source of power is waiting for us to acknowledge His divine existence and complete control of our souls. He is not interested in the traditional ways that seem to prolong the progress of His predestined purpose, but He is interested in the willingness of His creation to want Him as much as they want people to know them. The choice is ours to make and it's a simple one because there is no greater force that can dictate and bring to pass the original purpose of mankind. He wants you. Do you want Him? The decision is ours and life or death of the soul is the consequence of the choice we make.

The Essence of Life
Order Form

Postal orders: Wilco Family Partnership
19809-B North Cove Rd. Suite 207
Cornelius, NC 28031

Telephone orders: 704-895-6029

E-mail orders: williamskingskid@aol.com

Please send *The Essence of Life* **to:**

Name: _____

Address: _____

City: _____ State: _____

Zip: _____

Telephone: (____) _____

Book Price: $12.50

Shipping: $3.00 for the first book and $1.00 for each additional book to cover shipping and handling within US, Canada, and Mexico. International orders add $6.00 for the first book and $2.00 for each additional book.

Or order from:
ACW Press
5501 N. 7th. Ave. #502
Phoenix, AZ 85013

(800) 931-BOOK

or contact your local bookstore